Atlanta's
HALF-CENTURY

BOOKS BY FURMAN BISHER

With a Southern Exposure
Miracle in Atlanta
Strange but True Baseball Stories
Arnold Palmer: The Golden Years
Aaron
The College Game
The Masters
The Furman Bisher Collection
Thankful

BOOKS BY CELESTINE SIBLEY

The Malignant Heart
Peachtree Street USA
Dear Store
Christmas in Georgia
A Place Called Sweet Apple
Especially at Christmas
Mothers Are Always Special
The Sweet Apple Gardening Book
Day by Day with Celestine Sibley
Small Blessings
Children, My Children
Young 'Uns
For All Seasons
Jincey
Turned Funny
Tokens of Myself
A Plague of Kinfolks
Dire Happenings at Scratch Ankle
Straight as an Arrow
Ah, Sweet Mystery
The Celestine Sibley Sampler
Spider in the Sink

Atlanta's HALF-CENTURY

As seen through
the eyes of columnists
FURMAN BISHER
and
CELESTINE SIBLEY

LONGSTREET PRESS, INC.
Atlanta, Georgia

Published by
LONGSTREET PRESS, INC.
A subsidiary of Cox Newspapers
A subsidiary of Cox Enterprises, Inc.
2140 Newmarket Parkway, Suite 122
Marietta, GA 30067

The Furman Bisher columns about Arnold Palmer, Bobby Dodd and Ty Cobb appeared in *With a Southern Exposure*, 1962, Thomas Nelson & Sons. They are reproduced here verbatim from the newspaper.

The Furman Bisher columns about Bobby Jones, Hank Aaron, Ted Turner, Cliff Roberts and Bitsy Grant appeared in *The Furman Bisher Collection*, 1989, Taylor Publishing Company. They are reproduced here verbatim from the newspaper.

Printed by The Maple-Vail Book Manufacturing Group

1st printing 1997

Library of Congress Catalog Card Number: 97-76578

ISBN: 1-56352-460-0

Edited by Tom Bennett

Illustrated by Dale Dodson

Electronic Film Prep by OGI, Forest Park, GA
Jacket and book design by Burtch Hunter

To our mothers

Contents

In fancy journalism schools these days, they say they'll teach you the trade of newspapering. And some very good teachers in those places will spend time with students discussing the art of the interview, and how to organize paragraphs, and why adjectives matter. And this is, I suppose, a good thing.

But it is also true that some of the very best newspaper people are, quite simply, naturals. They are natural listeners and natural storytellers. They are naturally enthusiastic about life, and they come into newspapering because they couldn't imagine doing anything else. They know, without ever having to be told, a marvelous secret: Newspapering is the best job in the world.

Any newspaper is lucky if it has one of these writers. Any newspaper that has two is unnaturally blessed. Any newspaper that has had two working on the premises for as long as 50 years — well, now you're talking something extraordinary.

You can get technical on me and point out that Furman Bisher spent most of his years working for *The Atlanta Journal*, while Celestine Sibley spent most of her years working for *The Atlanta Constitution*, and for a long time those newspapers were fiercely competitive, even though owned by a single proprietor. (The day I met her, Celestine pointed out the window toward a big red heap of an abandoned building three blocks away — the former offices of the *Constitution* — and said, "That's where we were the day the *Journal* got us." She said it matter-of-factly, tinged with a bit of rancor and disbelief, as if the upstart *Journal's* purchase of the venerable morning paper had happened a week or so ago; in fact, at that point, the news was nearly 40 years old.)

Technicalities aside, the fact is that you can read them both now, cheek by jowl, in the Sports and Living sections of our daily newspaper, and it's about time somebody brought them together in a book.

The old *Journal* and *Constitution* rivalry reminds me of another characteristic of "natural" newspapermen and women: They are intensely loyal to the paper for which they work. They are always sure of its strengths and worried about its shortcomings. Thus Bisher is still, emphatically and always, a *Journal* person. He will call me to complain when the stock lists get screwed up in the evening edition, and he is the first to ask why the street final didn't carry such-and-such a story.

Sibley is still, first and foremost, a *Constitution* person; her computer rests beside Henry Grady's grand old roll-top desk, recently refurbished.

But it is to the benefit of readers that the gradual merger of our two titles and staff has brought both columnists into both papers, around the clock. After all these years, after the rivalries, after the *Journal* building on Forsyth Street was outgrown and we moved around the corner to Marietta Street, Furman Bisher and Celestine Sibley now have offices on the same floor, within shouting distance of each other.

They aren't always found there, of course; a columnist's stories come from life experienced outside the newspaper plant. But if you are lucky enough, you can ride the elevator with them both of a morning, and watch them greet each other. He'll say, "Good morning, Earnestine," referring to a long-ago luncheon speech in which she was introduced as "Earnestine Selby." And she'll say to him, "Good morning, Freeman," for his name was once similarly mangled as "Freeman Baker."

Then, happily, silently, their eyes cast dutifully upward, they'll rise toward the eighth floor and the day's work. Knowing full well that some of the youngsters in the elevator with them are thinking: "Why, those old fools; they don't even know their names!"

— John Walter
Managing Editor,
Atlanta Journal-Constitution

FURMAN BISHER

The Atlanta Constitution 1950-57
The Atlanta Journal 1957-82
The Atlanta Journal-Constitutution 1982 to present

A magnolia tree grew atop a bank in centerfield at old Ponce de Leon Park, a leafy eyewitness to the city's minor-league era. With tongue in cheek, Furman Bisher "interviewed" the tree in 1990. He termed his approach here "silly" in his last paragraph; in fact, it was a creative way to introduce new generations of readers to Atlanta's storied baseball past. This is a favorite column of his, about a favorite player who had a spirited name.

May 10, 1990
Remembering the old Crackers

- - - - -

(In the days of the Atlanta Crackers baseball club, a large magnolia tree stood in centerfield, on a terrace rising just above the playing level. Until the latter seasons at Ponce de Leon Park, when a scoreboard blocked it out, the tree was in play. Only Eddie Mathews, then a kid of 19, ever hit a ball into the tree, the story goes. I can confirm that, but I can't deny there may have been others.

In the season of 1956, the Crackers had a centerfielder named Jack Daniels, his real name, who was for one season the best centerfielder I've ever seen. Anywhere. He was the only one I ever remember running up a bank to make a catch under a magnolia tree.

Ponce de Leon Park is gone, the ground auctioned off 25 years ago.

Down the left-field line is a place called the Great Mall of China. In right field, where billboards rose in tiers, is a catering service. In center field, the old magnolia tree still stands, maybe a little larger, maybe not.

The other day I went out to see the tree. Litternuts had left Snickers wrappers, Kentucky Fried Chicken bags, McDonald's cartons, styrofoam cups beneath it, the stuff you see where America displays its bad manners. But we had a visit, the tree and I.)

Well, Tree, long time no see, or something like that. You still look the same, haven't changed a leaf. I know how us old guys like to hear that, but I mean it. You look like you could still go nine if they transplanted you to center field downtown in the stadium. And you might cover more ground than some we've had.

I tell people about you being the only tree I ever saw play centerfield in pro baseball, and they don't believe me. They should have been here

when you were in your prime and the Crackers were winning all those pennants. Don't be modest, you did your part. You were their 10th man long before anybody ever thought of the wretched DH.

(Don't ask me what that means. I can't even talk about DH without getting sick at my stomach.) I wonder, Tree, if you ever miss the old gang. Some of them are still around town. Bob Montag, the home run king, Buck Riddle, who hit a few himself, Dick Grabowski, Bob Sadowski. Don't see anything of Whitlow Wyatt anymore. He never leaves his county.

Mathews came through and managed the Braves and went, and Chuck Tanner, too. Both asked about you. I lied. I told them you were doing great. I didn't tell them I hadn't seen you in 20 years. Clyde King was through town the other day and I told him I'd just visited you. This time I wasn't lying.

I always guessed that if any of the old guys came to town and asked about you, it would be Jack Daniels. "Sour Mash," they called him. I always thought he was your closest friend, much time as you spent together around that terrace. Nobody could go up that rise and pull in a drive like he could. Then make the throw. Then come to the plate and give you as much action.

The season he played centerfield for Clyde King, Jack Daniels had the most curious set of stats I ever saw. He'd spent a season with the Braves, mostly doing defensive gigs and caddying for the big hitters.

When he got to Atlanta in '56, he was only 29 years old but he was on his way down. The season he had, Tree, was like one last shot of a Roman candle.

He led off, and was the most unusual leadoff hitter I ever saw. His time at bat was either a home run, a walk or a strikeout, it seemed. He hit 34 home runs, walked 143 times and struck out 113 times. Scored 126 runs, led the club in everything. In his 669 times at bat, he reached base 320 times, counting walks and hits, and that's nearly a .500 average.

Tree, you just didn't see that being done in those days. You should have appreciated him. You had the best view of any of us.

The last news I had of him wasn't good. While he consumed a good deal of the product whose name he bore, that wasn't his problem. He'd had part of a leg amputated because of some diabetic condition, and that's second-hand news. Tell you one thing, you could have Mantle or Mays or Reiser or any of those guys, but for one season with the glove, I take Jack Daniels.

I haven't asked you about your memories, but then I forget that trees don't talk, except in movie cartoons or Disneyland. If you could, you would tell me if Mathews was really the only guy who reached you with a drive.

Oh, there's a lot you could tell. Do the railroad men still wave when the train passes on the bank? Did the guys in the left-field bleachers really make bets on balls and strikes? Have you found happiness without the Crackers? I don't want any answers, Tree. Just let me get away from here before I get any sillier.

When something occurs in Sports that Furman Bisher considers unique, you can bet that it is. Such is the case with the 1950s race won, then lost, by Richard Petty. His own father ordered a recount and was declared the winner. A decade later, Petty won a $12,800 purse at Atlanta International Raceway, or about what some pro athletes make for a single game in the 1990s. "That's why the Pittsburgh Pirates are my favorite team," Bisher says. "The whole team isn't making as much as Greg Maddux."

Aug. 8, 1966
Poor Richard the Rich

- - - - -

HAMPTON, Ga. — Well, Richard Petty finally wins a stock car race in Georgia. Sandy Koufax wins a baseball game. Cassius Clay wins a fight. Richard Petty wins an automobile race. Big deal. Doesn't Richard Petty always win?

Everywhere but in Georgia. This state is a desert to the racing family from North Carolina. Petty had won at every big speedway in the South, but never in Georgia. Richard had taken home $52,000 in loot this year, but not a brownie from Georgia.

You name the bad news, it's happened to him around here. Blown engines, ruptured fuel lines, cracked blocks, busted tires. One race he used 32 tires and never finished. He left more rubber on the track than Firestone and Goodyear combined can make.

I forgot. One year he did win a race in Georgia. It was before the big tracks, though. And actually he didn't win it. For a little while, though, he was the winner.

You'd never guess who took it away from him — his daddy.

"You can't say a feller wins a race when he comes in second," Lee

Petty said, "so he didn't win, I did."

He was laughing about it now. You can laugh about something that ruffled your feathers eight or ten years ago, and Lee's feathers were ruffled that eight or ten years ago.

It happened at Lakewood Park. The old red dirt track still clung jealously to some of the fading grandeur at the time, but it was failing fast. Becoming a potholed dust bowl.

RICHARD PETTY

Richard was just a kid, about 20. Lee was a hard-nosed veteran stretching out every dime he could make. If you'd told him then that in 1966 he'd be running a race in Georgia for $12,800 first money, he'd have asked you if you escaped, or did they just let you out for the afternoon without your strait-jacket.

From all appearances, Richard had won the feature at Lakewood. Little boy winning his first race and his daddy second. Nice, warm American family story.

Naturally, dear old dad's going to grip son's hand, tell him how great it is and then the warm embrace. Father and son.

You prove it happened that way and I'll prove that Liz Taylor weighs 270 and plays left tackle for Green Bay. Dear old dad, Lee, that is, stomped up to the officials, such as they were in those days, fire in his eye and demanded a recount.

"You got the right family but the wrong winner," he said. "I was first. Richard was second."

They double-checked the laps. Lee was right. He'd won the race. Richard handed over the check, and what went with it, and Lee said, "Too bad, boy. When you win your first one, I want you to win it. I don't want it give to you."

Of course, that's all changed by now. Richard has won so many races that his daddy has all he can do to build cars for him. They're wealthy now, and $12,800 wealthier after Sunday afternoon at Atlanta International Raceway.

Richard won the Dixie 400, third and last in the year's series of races at A.I.R., and this time he sneaked up on it. It was a 400-mile race that started with Curtis Turner on everybody's mind and ended with Petty there instead and Turner on his way out of town.

This is one of the marvels of the age, Curtis Turner. He drove his first race when Petty was nine years old, and since that time everything good and bad has happened to him.

"Millionaire lumberman," they used to call him.

"That's right," Turner once said. "I'm a millionaire lumberman. I've got a million board-feet."

Made big money, was the man behind the building of Charlotte Speedway, banned by NASCAR, hit the dirt tracks and USAC, tried promoting, drifted out of sight, considered obsolete and over the hill.

Last year, Bob Colvin of Darlington Speedway got him reinstated by Bill France. You'd never believe it, but after being away from it that long and out of touch with the big tracks, Turner came back and won three races of stature.

Last week he wiped out Petty's qualifying record at A.I.R. and took the pole. Got to be 45 or 46, but still the male animal, tall and rugged like a Texas sheriff.

Sunday, retired drivers milled about the pits, Frank Mundy, Fonty Flock, Roscoe Thompson, Junior Johnson, to name a few.

"They're too old to drive," said Curtis, giving his nose a humorous tilt. "Take a kid like me that can stay up and frolic at night and come out bright and bushy-tailed. There's a lot of race in this ol' hoss yet."

For awhile Turner looked as young as his self-appraisal. He put that gold-and-black paint job, Fireball Roberts' old colors, out front and challenged the kids to come and get him.

They did. After 128 laps, Turner's Chevelle went behind the wall, and the race was left to the young society, Petty, Fred Lorenzen, Buddy Baker and Sam McQuagg, who is swifter than his name. "Out," said the track report of the car that daringly wears "13," "bad distributor." Turner changed clothes and disappeared.

It was left to Petty and Baker — Elzie Wylie Baker Jr., if you insist on formality — two kids who grew up in the pits while their daddies raced. But finally, Petty, outwitting his rival on pit stops, won it. He had to. After all this time, Georgia owed it to him.

To grasp just how long Furman Bisher has been a premiere golf writer, consider this memorable column. Bisher knew Arnold Palmer when the latter was a Wake Forest undergraduate, competing in the Southeast Intercollegiate in Athens. Later, at Palmer's first Masters' victory, the columnist could still only think of the new champion "in terms of a boy."

April 7, 1958
The positive thinker

- - - - -

AUGUSTA, Ga., April 7 — Precisely at the hour of 10:32 Easter Sunday morning, Arnold Palmer stepped up to the cashier's window at the Richmond Hotel and checked out, seven and one-half hours before he was to be suited out in a green sport jacket.

At the moment he was leg-locked in a tie with Sam Snead for the lead in the Masters golf tournament, a little festival near and dear to all golf players in this world.

"Isn't this a brash display of optimism?" a fellow asked Palmer.

"Positive thinking," said the golfer, winking with hearty good will, "just positive thinking."

Well, before the day was spent, and before Palmer scored his 73 and won the tournament, an abundance of positive thinking had been required. It happens that on this final round, Palmer is paired with Ken Venturi, who is hungering for a Masters championship like nobody else has ever hungered.

On the very first hole there is dramatic action. You see, actually not many people are thinking in terms of Palmer. He is a young fellow, he has been playing in tournaments and he has won more tournaments in 1957 than any other professional. He won at Houston, at Wilmington, at Akron and at San Diego.

But he is still Arnold Palmer, and he is not a notable figure among the professionals. Besides, as a man who can remember him as an undergraduate at Wake Forest, when Jim Weaver was driving the car and signing the tabs for the golf team, you can only think of him in terms of a boy.

Venturi, who is three strokes behind Snead and Palmer, is charging the field, and he comes into the first hole with a recovery shot that leaves him 35 or 40 feet from the cup. Venturi sinks his putt stylishly.

ARNOLD PALMER

Snead comes along a few minutes later and he takes a humbling six on the same hole, and so your arithmetic shows you that Venturi has picked up three strokes on one of the leaders on the first hole.

But nobody really is thinking of Palmer. They are thinking of Snead as the leader, and as the guy Venturi has got to beat.

Pretty soon Snead has blown it. It is like 1951, when he went into the last round tied with Skee Riegel for the lead, and when he works feverishly over a cool 80, and Ben Hogan wins it.

"I never drove so well and scored as bad in my life," Snead said when he arrived in the clubhouse. He was in a good humor, and there was no bitterness. What he couldn't control was his long irons, and these golf players tell you that the most important shot on most any hole is the second shot, which is usually a long iron or a mid-iron.

Well, the Venturi and Palmer twosome makes the turn and Venturi has picked up a stroke on Palmer. You can sense that the nice, young Californian is about to make his move. He is determined to win this thing, and he has started the day three strokes behind Palmer and Snead.

I guess that if you get to a turning point, you begin at the 12th hole. This is a par three, and this is where the controversy comes up, almost a baseball-style controversy in which the players and the umpires come to a crisis.

Palmer overshoots the green and the ball lands in a muddy bank, almost buried out of sight. There is a consultation. Rules committeemen come up and they have a look, and they look at one another and say, "Well, what do you think of this?"

Finally, one of them turns to Venturi and says, "What do you think of this? Should Palmer have to play the imbedded ball, or drop one and play it?"

Venturi says, "Well, I think he ought to be allowed to drop one and play it, but I hope he has to play the imbedded ball."

He wants to win the tournament.

The rules committee, after a meeting at the summit, finally let Palmer play the imbedded ball, on which he scores a five, and then let him play a provisional ball, on which he scores a three.

Nobody knows anything, especially five or six thousand people in the gallery. By the time Venturi and Palmer and their gallery reach the 15th fairway, they get the official decision. Palmer is allowed a three instead of a five on No. 12, and these are the strokes by which he wins the tournament.

Of course, since that time the stout Wake Forest alumnus scored an eagle on No. 13, and these two strokes also win it for him. He has come out of a tough clinch, like a game prize fighter, and he has the hardy facial features of a prize fighter.

Palmer goes on and he scores his 73 and a 284 and he looks pretty safe. But he is not safe yet until Doug Ford and Fred Hawkins, who are playing in a twosome, have both missed long putts on No. 18 when either one could have sunk it and tied Palmer.

Palmer is dressed out in his new green coat in the ceremony on the practice green and it is all over. There is a lot of history in the press tent, where Palmer tells about himself, because he is still mostly a stranger.

His daddy is the professional at a nine-hole course in Latrobe, Pa., and this is still his home. "When I get in trouble with my game," he said, "my daddy is still the one I run to. I go home and he works on my game. I've been nothing but a golf player since I was five years old, and I've been waiting for a day like this."

He won the National Amateur one year, and now he wins this. No other national amateur champion has ever won the Masters before. I keep thinking of Ford, who had predicted that he would win, and Venturi who had thought he would win. But the most positive thinker of all was Arnold Palmer, who checked out of his hotel room Sunday morning, and he won.

Bobby Dodd Sr. coached Georgia Tech. His son, Bobby Dodd Jr., was a backup quarterback for Florida. Ray Graves, Dodd Sr.'s former aide, coached Florida. Alice Dodd, wife and mother, sat in the stands unsure who to root for. "They all came together in one big collision of family, heart and sentiment," Bisher recalls. On this afternoon, "the ending was too unreal for anyone to attempt in fiction."

Oct. 3, 1960
Too real for Hollywood

- - - - -

Mounting the stadium steps at Florida Field in Gainesville, Fla., Saturday came a broad, bulky man. When he reached a row high in the stands, about the 37-yard line, he turned off and sat down in seat No. 15.

He wore a broad smile on his face and warmly greeted several people sitting in his neighborhood. It may have been a mask of congeniality he was wearing, but it appeared to be real.

Then he sat down and waited for the show to start, and when it did, he was entertained by two hours and 20 minutes of the gol-darndest crop of football he ever expected to see.

University of Florida defeated Georgia Tech, 18-17, and in the course of it, George Robert Woodruff, holder of seat No. 15, high up on the 37-yard line, saw what they wanted of him at Florida, why he was discarded as the head coach and replaced by Ray Graves.

Wild, daring, gambling, reckless, frenzied, sometimes foolish football took place.

I have a feeling that it wouldn't have made a great lot of difference to the Gator Growlers if quarterback Larry Libertore and fullback Jon MacBeth had missed on the two-point conversion that won the game with 32 seconds left. It was assuring enough that they'd gone for it.

It was the signature of a new regime, a regime that would gamble. It may have been the beginning of a new era in football at Florida.

I say this with the trace of boos that replaced the uproar after the touchdown sounding on my memory. Graves said there had never been any doubt about going for the two-pointer. Yet, somehow or another, Billy Cash, his sophomore end who placekicks, got onto the field when it was time for the conversion.

BOBBY DODD SR.

Georgia Tech called time out, and when the respite was over, Florida lined up to run off a two-point play that Libertore made up himself on the field.

Whatever decision anyone of responsibility might have made on the sideline at this time, he could have been slightly excused had he erred.

The finish was utterly absurd. No self-respecting movie firm would look twice at such a manuscript, the coach's sophomore son helping his father's former chief assistant beat his father in the dying moments of the son's first big game on his own campus. Too obvious.

The Dodd angle, Bobby Sr. and Bobby Jr., had been whipped to a froth in the buildup. Next to nothing was expected to come of it, really.

That the outcome should linger in doubt until such a point, and that young Dodd should figure so prominently in the resolving of the issue in such a snake-pit of seething emotion was simply carrying the thing too far.

There's no removing Libertore from his pedestal. He was the climactic force. But it was Dodd Jr. who bodily lifted the ox out of the ditch on the drive to the touchdown that won. The Gators had been thrown back to their 42-yard line. The down was third with 19 yards to go.

Dodd Jr. was rushed aboard with a play. He dropped straight back and lofted a pass that halfback Don Deal caught at Tech's 25 for a 33-yard gain.

There was to be no retreat for the Gators now. They had the emotional impetus and they moved on in, but not without the aid of Dodd Jr. again. He ran a quarterback sneak for a first down at the three, then recovered a fumble at the very door to the end zone, saving it all.

It was an exhilarating triumph for him, and he went off to his Saturday night date in good humor. His father maintained a stout front at all times, but the defeat cut him deeply. This was twice in the same season he had been defeated by a former assistant, in the Gator Bowl by Frank Broyles, and now by Graves, abetted by his own son.

For Alice Dodd, wife and mother, it was even worse. Besieged by magazine photographers throughout the day, eavesdropped upon by snooping reporters who infiltrated the stands around her, and stared at like a curiosity, she was ripped to emotional shreds. It's almost inhuman to put a woman through such an ordeal.

The Georgia Tech team could have saved Mrs. Dodd a good deal of grief. The Jackets played the first quarter as if in a trance. They were sluggish. They moved lead-footedly downfield on punts and kickoffs, until they found they were in for a furious fight.

They never really got with it in the manner of which they seem capable. But perhaps they were only suffering by comparison beside the dedicated Gators, who attacked in the suicidal manner of a wave of Japanese banzai troops. They, the Gators, subsisted on effort and determination beyond human limitations.

Yet, they were never ahead until the last 32 seconds. Let this be said for them, though. In this frenetic moment of football, when all strategy and tactic seemed more the product of happenstance than plan, they never strayed so far from the realm of reason as to lose sight of the most desirable stage at which to be in front.

Ty Cobb came home to die. Bisher went to see him, and the Georgia Peach reflected on his battles with the other giants of baseball's golden era. Later, on Cobb's death, Bisher had to reconstruct his notes quickly as he dictated this to The Journal sports department. It became one of his most memorable columns.

July 18, 1961
Complex in the manner of great men

- - - - -

HILTON HEAD ISLAND, S.C., July 18 — The news that Ty Cobb had died reached Hilton Head early Monday afternoon, and by sundown it was the most reverently discussed topic among the clientele of the William Hilton Inn, gathered in clots by poolside, in the little red-leather lounge and in the dining room. He had not struck a home run, or stolen a base, or filed a spike in 33 years. But this was the kind of hold the man had on the public.

The news of death came as no shock. It had been expected for several days. Yet the realization that the Georgia Peach was no longer among the living created a strange emptiness.

Whatever one feels for such a man as Cobb, be it respect, awe, or idolatry, it is tempered at such moments by the realization that there is no immortality. Only the records exist now to preserve the name in a perspective that will vary with the erosive effects of the years that will come to pass.

Rememberances are aroused. You see him in many settings and in many moods, at the table of his dining room in California, at home plate in Ponce de Leon Park, in a hotel room in New York City, but most vivid of them all is the memory of him in the living room in the ante-bellum home in Cornelia.

He had come back to Georgia to build a home on the top of Chenocetah Mountain. He was drifting about in obvious uncertainty. A sentimental plot was bedded in his mind, but impeded by an unwillingness to shut himself off in self-appointed isolation.

"I'm tired," he said, sinking into an easy chair in the home he had rented while he contemplated his plans.

"I'm old and I'm tired. I don't like to say I'm old, but I am. It has been a tough life, 24 years of fighting off Lajoie, Jackson, Collins, Speaker and Ruth. Trying to stay ahead of them. I had to do that era after era."

This was the utterance that smote you. I remember I sat up straight with surprise. This was a moment that I marked in my life as rich history.

TY COBB

He talked on. I didn't dare breathe heavily fearing I'd damage the entranced declaration of a great man's inner thoughts.

"I've used myself up since I was 17. I don't believe any player had a tougher time of it in baseball than I did. Now I'm 71 and tired and I want to get out of circulation. I'm going to be hard to find on my mountain."

From the top of the mountain the next day he pointed down to a house that sat small and plain in the valley. About where the settlement of Narrows used to be.

"Down there," he said, "in that little valley is the house where I was born. Not that one, but one close by. No one lives in it now, but it's still standing."

The smoke curled up from the chimney of the house in view and flattened out over the valley. You could imagine the baby child in the arms of his mother, remembered in those parts as a raven-haired beauty, and you looked at this soul-weary man beside you searching for something he couldn't reach. A baby had gone out from that wilderness to the greatest fame an athlete could know, and you wondered what it could possibly be that he still sought.

It must have been something to fight for again. When he was on his mountain, there was nothing left but to sit and look down, on his Georgia. This was rewarding in sentimental value but low in the measurement of self-achievement.

When he went away, he enjoyed notoriety, but when he went away he wanted to be back. He was fighting this battle to the death. There would never have been a truce.

It is for others to write of his battles on the field as a Detroit Tiger and Philadelphia Athletics player. Some of the motivating forces fascinate more in the study of Cobb the aggressor.

All such men as this are complex. They never merely resort to emotion. They employ it until it soon overwhelms them. Cobb could be deeply sentimental. "I can cry," he once told me. "It runs in the family."

He could be vindicative, patronizing, arrogant, soft, violent, dramatic; but his emotional range never included apathy. What he felt at the moment, he felt with a passion that set him afire.

As he grew older, he grew more dedicated to the memory of his father, an educator and legislator from Royston. "My father was a man devoted to education," he said. "He was a school teacher, and a superintendent of county schools, then a state senator. He wanted to get me in position to get an appointment to Annapolis, but I had my mind set on baseball. My mind was made up."

"My father's devotion to education, that was the spark. That and the fact that I never went to college..." This is how he explained his establishment of the Cobb Educational Foundation for worthy but financially unqualified young men and women of Georgia.

He sat on the front porch swing of the Cobb home until 3 o'clock in the morning, arguing his case of baseball against his father's case for education, in the day of his youth. Finally, his father gave in. The next day, young Ty left for Augusta.

Another front porch scene took place in Royston many months later. Ty was on his way to Detroit now, called to the major leagues. His father lay a corpse in the funeral home. Ty listened to the story of how he died, accidentally shot by his mother. Fire burned in his eyes and the words he spoke were inflammable. He would go out and get even with the world for this cruel stroke.

This was the activator. This drove him to play his fierce game. The ability was God-given. This was the force behind it.

Hotamitey! Junior Johnson is no different from any other good old boy born and raised in Wilkes County, N.C. That's not all. Chickens have heads for counting, just like cows and horses. So penned Bisher in this hilarious send-up of Tom Wolfe's 1965 Esquire *magazine article about Johnson and the colorful world of NASCAR.*

June 10, 1965
This feller wore a vest

- - - - -

HAMPTON, Ga. — Junior Johnson and all the good old boys were back in town Wednesday, making more racket than six mules running loose in a kitchenware shop, and shaping up for the big automobile race on Sunday.

Their union-alls were hung by the NASCAR trailer with care, in hope that St. Nelson Weaver soon would be there, bearing money and other goodies.

Used to be, the best a stock car racing driver could expect out of Atlanta was a snootful of dust and a bumpy afternoon over the ruts of old Lakewood Park. But we've gone bigtime now, and the good old boys who come here are the ones who hit all the big towns in the South, like Bristol, North Wilkesboro, Daytona, Martinsville, Darlington, Hampton — members of the road show playing the circuit.

It's sort of odd, what it takes to make a man a catbird. He may have been doing the same thing he's been doing for all these years, never changing his style or habits, and never realizing that he was any different from the next one. Maybe he's Junior Johnson, heavy-set, stone-chinned, moon-faced, grey-dappled hair, about as plain and average a good old country boy as you'll find around Wilkes County, N.C.

In fact, you see one feller from Wilkes County, you've just about seen them all.

Then one day a fancy story writer blows in from New York, smelling sweet and prissy like that stuff they use at the barber shop. He's wearing a vest, and there's a piece of hair hanging carelessly down his forehead.

People ain't seen a vest around Wilkes County since the last funeral they went to. You bury the oldtimers in them, but you don't wear the danged things anymore.

"It's so hot it'd melt the fillings in ye teeth," Junior Johnson said, "and here comes this feller in town wearing a vest. And a wool coat. Wearing a vest and a wool coat.

"I reckon he musta come around off and on for a year. I'd be talking to somebody somewheres, and I'd look over my shoulder, and there'd be this funny little guy from New York wearing the vest and listening.

"You know that picture they run, of me drinking a Coke in the store at Ingle Holler? I was just standing there drinking that Coke one day, and I heard this click, and I turned around and there was this feller with the vest and a photographer."

The funny little feller with the vest had come down from New York City to write a story about Robert Glenn (Junior) Johnson, former specialist in moonshine logistics, now race car driver.

By the time he got through, he had made moonshining seem right respectable and Junior Johnson sound like a hillbilly knight in Blue Bell overalls.

The little man's name was Tom Wolfe, vest and all. Not any kin to the Wolfes over in Asheville, and that Tom. This is a New York Wolfe.

Not even a sportswriter, but a Ph.D., which wouldn't cut any ice in Wilkes County, N.C. You put Ph.D. after somebody's name in Wilkes County and they'll think it's a misprint for RFD.

Good old Tom wrote one of the great magazine stories about Junior Johnson, plain, old-shoe Junior Johnson. His kind get born every day up in Wilkes County, grow up, live their lives and then die and never get heard of outside of Ingle Hollow, Miller's Creek or Ronda.

Old Junior had been driving these cars around race tracks for years, winning some races and attracting a modest following of admirers. But you spoke of stock car racing around the beer taverns and at the drive-in places, and people always brought up Fireball Roberts, or Lee Petty, and a little later, Freddie Lorenzen. Not Junior Johnson.

Now, all of a sudden, Junior Johnson had become somebody. *Esquire* magazine put Tom Wolfe's story up close to the front, with all that photography and all that writing about the good old boys, and Sunday afternoon at the track in North Wilkesboro, and the big Coca-Cola sign.

Hotamitey, Junior Johnson had become an international personality, all on account of the funny little guy wearing the vest.

JUNIOR JOHNSON

"We've had people come around from all over the world just to get a look at Junior—from Australia, England, South Africa, all over the world. Just to get a look at Junior."

Fred Lovett was talking. Fred is a good old boy, too, sort of big around the middle, but a big frame to go with it. Easy natured. Man of money, but not advertising it with fancy silk suits and big diamond rings.

Fred Lovett is Holly Farms Industries. This is a dude name for a chicken slaughterhouse. You've seen that red sign on the side of Junior's race car. Junior works for him.

I don't mean chicken-plucking, and all that. "Public relations," Fred said. He grinned a little. "Junior comes by the office once in awhile. To work on his car."

"Where is Holly Farms located, sir?"

"All over Wilkes County," Fred Lovett said. He made a big circle with his hands. "Yeah, all over Wilkes County. We got ten million head of chicken, process a million a week."

"Head? I thought that was for cows and horses."

"Chickens got heads, ain't they?" Fred said.

"Has all this notoriety gone to Junior's head? I mean...."

"Naw. Some of the home folks look at him a little strange, but most of them up there ain't even read it," Fred said. "Nobody got any copies of *Esquire* magazine in Wilkes County. It got him talked about and made him a character, but it won't change ol' Junior."

Good old Junior grinned that sort of sidesaddle grin of his. "They sure write weird stuff in that *Esquire* magazine, anyway," he said. "Not just that little feller with the vest, but all of 'em."

While on the way to a dove shoot with then-Governor Jimmy Carter, Bisher learned of the death of Bobby Jones. "Of all the athletes who have competed on the face on this earth, regardless of the game or the continent, the one untarnishable image was that of Bob Jones," Bisher wrote, and that estimate has not changed in the years since. A "cleek" mentioned here "is a cut-down club, something between a two-iron and a putter," he says.

Dec. 20, 1971
The gentleman athlete

- - - - -

The final decisive humbling of man is death. It comes to each and all in various manners, and sometimes the lowly are redeemed in the end by dying heroically, and sometimes those of highest dignity are brought to their passing by the most excruciating of forms.

Several years ago, and I am not certain of the year for it is unimportant now, Robert Tyre Jones Jr. and I sat and talked of life and philosophy and great moments until we finally arrived at a discussion of the ailment which had so violently disabled him.

"What is the nature of it?" I asked him.

"The medical name for it is *syringomyelia*," he said. "I call it pure hell."

"Is there any cure for it?"

"Oh, yes," he said.

"What is it?" I asked.

There was a brief pause. Then he said, "Death."

Saturday morning, while I was heading toward Swainsboro for a dove shoot with Governor Jimmy Carter, Bob Jones finally got "the cure." In the most devastating, excruciating of forms. Drawn, withered, shrunken, cruelly stripped of all the dramatic coordination that created of him the most celebrated player of golf in all these centuries of our universe, death finally, mercifully arrived.

The one faculty spared him to the final stroke was his brilliance of mind. Never ever, during the whole siege that seized upon him and never relented, did that great man lose one ounce of his mental presence, for which some great power unknown to us all is to be given grateful thanks.

BOBBY JONES

Any attempt to describe Bob Jones to a world whose people respond to the name is squandered effort. There is no vouching for this story, and frankly I doubt the authenticity of it, but many years ago it was related to me.

Some great hunter invading darkest Africa supposedly came upon this tribe and was confronted by the chieftain. This hunter, being from Atlanta, discovered to his relief that the chieftain was conversant in English and explained to him that he came from the United States.

"Atlanta, Georgia," he said.

"Ot-lawnta, Geo-ghia," said the chieftain, and a light flashed on in the dark man's face. "Ah, Bobby Jones and Coca-Cola."

Of all the athletes who have competed on the face of this globe, regardless of the game or the continent, the one untarnishable image was that of Bob Jones. The one supreme player, whether he struck golf balls, punted footballs, pitched baseballs, smote tennis balls, kicked soccer balls, attacked wild animals or climbed mountain peaks, was Bob Jones.

The one ultimate ambition of all athletes, also regardless of his game, was to be regarded in that game as Bob Jones was in his.

I have no accounting for the number of columns and magazine stories I have written on other golfers. But to a man, all of them appear to have been inspired to be another Bob Jones.

Arnold Palmer, as he stood across that creek that coursed through the grounds where his father was the professional, said to himself as a boy, "I am Bobby Jones and this shot is for the national championship."

When Jack Nicklaus set a goal for himself, it was to exceed Jones's record of 13 major championships. And that's only skimming the cream off the top.

The most fascinating story I ever became involved with was that of Bob Jones's first exposure to golf. It was bound to have happened one way or another, I'm certain, but to my mind, one of life's most unrewarded men was the anonymous fellow who took the cleek out of his bag at old East Lake Country Club and bestowed it upon the child Jones.

East Lake in those times was a summer colony to which Atlanta families repaired in the hot season. It was 10 miles from downtown and a long street-car ride. The Jones family lived in a boarding house operated by a Mrs. Meador.

"One of the tenants," Bob once told me, "was a man named Fulton Colville, a member of the club who played golf. I followed him about a good deal, as children will, but I had no interest in golf. I was only six or seven years old."

"One day he gave me an old cleek out of his bag. It was much too long for me. My father took it over to Jimmy Maiden at the pro shop and Jimmy sawed it off and put a grip on it for me. I dug a hole in the top of a little hill and began playing up and down the street with it. Those were the days when you could turn a child loose in the streets, and that was how I was introduced to golf."

He was born in an old residence across from Grant Park, delivered by a family doctor named Kendrick. In those days, nobody was born in hospitals. He was an only child, sickly in the early years, but obviously the object around which his father orbited, for they came to enjoy a remarkable relationship.

He was bred to good manners and gracious living. Throughout his life he successfully depicted the term "gentleman." He was, in truth, THE gentleman athlete as the term originated.

Any attempt at this stage to refer to his magical career as a player is meaningless. There are others who could write of him with more authority than I, and the first who comes to mind is Ed Miles, retired golf historian of The *Journal*. I have always felt a dread of the day I would have to write editorially of the death of Bob Jones, and feel now an utter futility in the effort. Such is the fate of great men who achieve in one age and are left in death to the mercy of another. But in the case of Bob Jones his was a being that refers to all ages, and shall forever more.

It was the custom of the members of the Atlanta Classic Foundation to sing "some silly song" to the tournament winner afterwards in the locker room, Bisher recalls. However, he thought he sensed a special gusto in their singing in 1973, so pleased were they that at last a big-name player like Jack Nicklaus had won Atlanta's stop on the PGA tour.

May 28, 1973
A classic Atlanta Classic winner

- - - - -

The way I look at it, Jack Nicklaus ought to buy his own golf tour and play people like Superman, Atlas, Ben Hur, Paul Bunyan, Frank Merriwell and Perry Mason — those guys who swashed and buckled through life and legend making a travesty out of victory. At least get off the track and give some of the other players a chance to have some fun once in awhile like average mortals.

That's the only thing he hasn't got, his own tour. Otherwise, Nicklaus, sometimes known as the "Golden Bear" and not just for the color of his hair, is the golfer who has everything. He has more ways of getting to the purse than anybody since Titanic Thompson. Only his are honest.

He designs courses, from Spain to Japan. He has contracts with clothing manufacturers whose designs dictate what the well-dressed patron of the course shall wear. An 18-handicapper may not be able to play like Jack Nicklaus, but he can dress like him. He has stock in a firm that makes playing equipment. He has his own tournament management operation, Executive Sports Inc., which is John (Moose) Montgomery, and one of its several accounts is the Atlanta Classic, paying $150,000.

In other words, Nicklaus not only won the tournament and its first prize, which is $30,000, but he also drew a fee, indirectly, for directing it. Then there was all that equipment and all those clothes that bear his label or endorsement that was being sold around the Atlanta Country Club acres.

He DIDN'T design the course. He just played it like he did. By the end of the first three rounds of the Atlanta Classic, Nicklaus had shot himself so far out of sight you couldn't see him even from second place without a telescope. His rounds were 67-66-66, six strokes up on another alum of Ohio State University, Tom Weiskopf.

Sunday was reserved for the formality of playing the fourth round. Some of us suspected that the Classic would be just as well off to let the other pros move on to Charlotte and ask Jack to play the 18 on exhibition.

Well, it didn't quite work out to be such a ho-hummer as it might have been. The old ACC course rose up and got back some of its respectability. How dare this cad, no matter how immortal he be, strip the place of all its virtue!

It wasn't a picture day for golf, in the first place. The day broke wet and foreboding. The clouds boiled around and thunder rumbled occasionally, like a giant with a growling stomach. Rain would drop in occasional spits and mists.

All sorts of witchy things were happening. Somebody had stolen one of the concessions tents during the night. A security officer, or a likely impostor, drove up to a storage location, said 12 cases of beer were needed out on the course, loaded them up and was never seen again.

Weiskopf's second shot of the day struck a lady of the gallery in the head. She had to be rushed to a hospital. He had a bogey.

Just to show you how things were going for Golden Bear, though, his approach struck a woman among the gallery at the fifth hole, but the ball bounced off her shoulder back onto the green. Nicklaus knocked the putt in for a birdie, saving himself at least two, maybe three shots.

"It could have been the difference in the tournament," he said later, "as it turned out."

He had gone out on the course obviously not in pursuit of another record. With a six-stroke lead, a fellow could afford a yawn or two. He had to keep kicking himself to remind himself that this was a business round, and not one of those corporate outings. That this was PGA, not the ACC Memorial Day dogfite.

Nicklaus three-putted the ninth hole. He hit a trap on the 10th. He bogeyed the 12th. He had used 20 strokes to play four holes. He had his own undivided attention now, for just in front of him, Weiskopf was rediscovering the birdie. The lead was down to three strokes.

It had been the kind of circumstance at the outset in which even the maligned Tommy Aaron would have been forgiven for playing for second place (had he not missed the cut). But now, here was Weiskopf with a chance at the $30,000. Let Golden Bear make one miscalculation and we might have had an all Ohio-State playoff. This was not on Executive Sports Inc.'s tournament agenda.

JACK NICKLAUS

Nicklaus got hold of himself now and played it on in par, to put an end to your breathless suspense, and won just another golf tournament, to him. To the Classic, though, it was its first classic winner, and his nameplate on the big trophy becomes a matter of treasured prestige.

In fact, when it was all done, the presentation, the press tent surgery, the tape recordings, the autographs, and Nicklaus finally was able to flee to the refuge of the locker room, there stood orange-coated members of the Atlanta Classic Foundation, those men who underwrite it, in choral disarray singing, "For He's a Jolly Good Fellow."

And they meant it, backing up the endorsement with a few bubbles of champagne.

The prize represented the 176,064th dollar Nicklaus has won this year, the 1,878,769th of his career, merely on the golf course. It was his fourth tournament championship in less than six months.

More than anything else, it meant something extra to the Atlanta Classic. It's always a matter of pride to have a classic winner as if it took some master player to beat your course. Nicklaus and Gary Player had come close. The Classics were delighted to have Tommy Aaron win it. It gushed with sentiment. They were a little stunned when Bob Lunn slipped in again last year. I mean, you're only programmed for one Bob Lunn in your master plan. But Nicklaus — ah, sweet glory.

I won't say you'd find the same enthusiasm among the losing players. "The way big Jack's playing," said long George Archer. "He'll bring back the handicap system to pro golf."

In an Atlanta-Fulton County Stadium press box crammed with the world's press, Bisher searched for a unique angle on Hank Aaron's feat of breaking Babe Ruth's all-time home run record. The columnist found it, tracing the list of Hammerin' Hank's pitching victims. They ranged from Vic Raschi to "a Brewer, a Boozer and a Barr... three different Jacksons, and Veale and Lamb."

April 9, 1974
Aaron hits No. 715

- - - - -

The flower of American sporting journalism was caught with its tongue tied. With its fingers arthritic. Its brain turned into a glob of quivering gelatine. Its nervous system drawn as tight as a banjo's strings.

It had rehearsed every move, memorized every line. Then took the stage to perform and every word stuck in its throat.

Henry Louis Aaron hit the 715th home run in the 2,967th game of his major league career, and nobody had anything left to say. I mean, there just aren't 715 ways to say that Henry Aaron hit a home run. Besides, they'd worn out all the others in a long winter's anticipation, and last week when he hit No. 714 in Cincinnati.

In fact, No. 715 was only a rerun of No. 693, also hit off Al Downing in Atlanta Stadium with a man on base. And it was nothing to compare with No. 400, which cleared everything in Philadelphia and came down somewhere near Trenton. Aaron's guest of honor that night was Bo Belinsky.

There is this to be said about it: It was the first home run he has ever hit after hearing Pearl Bailey sing the national anthem. It was also an occasion added to extensively, though witlessly, by the absence of Bowie Kuhn, riotously referred to as the Commissioner of Baseball.

It was a Louisville bat against a Spalding ball, which hit a

BankAmerica sign over the left-field fence and was fielded by a left-handed pitcher named Tom House. Fifty-three thousand people saw it in person, but what they weren't going to appreciate so much was when they got home they learned that with their tickets their sellout had bought free television for the other million and a half Atlantans who stayed at home.

HANK AARON

The Braves had thrown open the show for local consumption just before the field was turned into a riot of color, Americana, teary-eyed emotionalism, political swashbuckling and deafening fireworks.

Alphonse Erwin Downing has won a Babe Ruth World Series for Trenton, N.J., and pitched in a World Series for the New York Yankees. He has won 115 games, 20 in one season, and become known as a steady, reliable member of the Los Angeles Dodgers. But Monday night he carved his initials on America's memory.

He has a new cross to bear. He won't be remembered for the 115 games, but for the inside fast ball that Aaron hit over the fence.

At the same time, he assured several pitchers of a place in posterity, a little hall of notoriety of their own. They all belong to the "We Served Henry Aaron a Home Run Club," senior member Vic Raschi, then on the shady side of a substantial career and serving it out as a St. Louis Cardinal.

The lineup of Aaron's victims is a procession of extremes, from Sandy Koufax, who was on his way to the Hall of Fame, to Joe Trimble, a Pittsburgh rookie who never won a game in the majors.

He hit No. 10 off Corky Valentine, who now may be seen around town as a cop. Then, he was a Cincinnati Red.

He hit one off an infielder, Johnny O'Brien, one of a pair of famous college basketball twins who was trying to discover a new career with the Pirates. He hit one off a Congressman, the Honorable Wilmer Mizell (R-NC). Wilmer was then "Vinegar Bend," a bumpkin rookie with a bashful smile and the kind of "Aw, shucks!" personality that made sports reporters look him up.

He hit another off Faul and off Law, and another off a Brewer, a Boozer and a Barr. One off Rabe and one off Mabe. And off Hook and Nye.

He hit 'em off Morehead and Moorhead. And R. Miller and R. L. Miller, three different Jacksons, and Veale and Lamb.

With No. 715 he assured permanent attention for handservants merely passing that way. Otherwise Thornton Kipper, Herb Moford, John Andre, Rudy Minarcin, Tom Acker, Lino Dinoso, Art Ceccarelli and the improbable Whammy Douglas would have passed on and been forgotten. They are now forever engraved on the marble of Aaron's record like the roll of the soldiers memorialized on a courthouse monument.

Naturally, one is supposed to feel that he has been witness to one of the monumental sports events of all history, if he were in the park. These things don't penetrate the perspective so soon. You're over-prepared. It's not like sitting there watching this flippant youth, Cassius Clay, knock a bear like Sonny Liston out of the world heavyweight title. Or Centre College whip Harvard.

There's no shock to get your attention. No. 715 was anticipated, awaited like childbirth. It's like buying a ticket to watch a bank get robbed, or a train wreck. Everybody's so thoroughly ready that nobody can appreciate the history of it all. Even the President sat in Washington with his dialing finger exercised for action.

"He invited me to the White House," Aaron said. It is suggested that he not loiter on the way.

"Magnavox gets the ball and the bat for five years, then they go to the Hall of Fame," he said. That covered several other loose ends.

I don't want to fuel still another fire, but as I depart I feel compelled to leave with you another record in the line of fire: Aaron is well ahead of Ruth's pace the year of his 60 home runs. The Babe didn't hit his second home run until the 11th game.

The "Chicago Twelve" passed the torch of Braves ownership to Ted Turner. In Bisher's words, he is "our society's true-blue 24-carat version of a sportsman." Turner's cost: about $12 million, a tremendous bargain. "I would estimate they are worth close to $200 million now," Bisher says.

Jan. 15, 1976
Ted Turner steps forth
- - - - -

Resplendent in his Henry Aaron cravat and tattersall vest, everything that's dapper down to the neatly tonsured mustache, Robert Edward Turner III bestowed local ownership upon the Atlanta Braves Tuesday. For a price, which by the time the debt is closed will come to something like $12 mllion, I'm told.

He's buying the franchise permitting him to operate in the National League the same way you bought your car, or the new bedroom furniture. A little bit down and so much per month.

Somebody once said that if you have to buy a Rolls-Royce on the installment plan, you not only don't need it, you can't afford it. Ted Turner has decided that he can afford it and Atlanta needs it.

"There's a civic side to my interest in the Braves," he said. "Economically, you know it's not a wise move in these times, but money is not the prime motivation."

At last he doesn't have to listen again to the sermon about if you're trying to make money, don't buy a sports franchise. And I hope he has noticed that owning a franchise looks even less profitable now that a man named Peter Seitz has just taken target practice with the reserve clause and shot it full of holes. There is the chance, you see, that Turner and his communications empire have bought rights to forty guys who'll be packing up and leaving town next October.

Emancipated "slaves."

But that's just part of the routine of learning to be the owner of a sports franchise. Way the dice roll. The cookie crumbles. Tough stuff, kid.

TED TURNER

Somehow, it isn't easy accustoming my vision to Ted Turner sitting between Dan Donahue and Bill Bartholomay, wearing dress-up clothes and looking dullishly executive. He has always played with boats, not ballplayers and bubble-gum cards. I'm accustomed to him at the helm, wearing his yachtsman's cap, salt spray tinging the gold leaf with a Silas Marner hue of green. Shouting order. Secure the poop deck and ready about, mate!

He has sailed in everything from the Swiss Navy to the Chattahoochee fleet. Anything that'll float and have a chance to win a race. He is, fellow Americans, our society's true-blue 24-carat version of a sportsman. That is, you win, you get paid off with a jug or a plaque.

This is a different tack. You get paid off with a bottom line, red or black. You don't have a grandstand floating along at sea. Your cheers are the self-satisfaction you get from leaving your wake for some lubber to follow.

That works two ways. Neither do you get the boos and the accursed letters to the editor.

Turner's ownership of the Braves creates a unique condition — a man in the communications business depending on rivals to spread the word of his product, and his good works, or otherwise, in baseball. New York was vast enough to swallow and digest CBS's ownership of the Yankees without a burp. Atlanta is still small-town enough that a small claw can make a large scratch. The rivalries carry some heat. How does the Channel 5 editorial voice come on the air ripping the Channel 17 owner's operation of the Braves?

Not to be neglected in this hour of transition is the retreating ownership. Trying to put a handle on terms to describe the tenure of the Chicago Twelve in the city isn't easy. Perhaps it's best that they sign out. Ten years of winning 797 and losing 815 hasn't endeared them to the territory.

They came in a heat wave of affection. They bow out in a wave of apathy. They tried. They really tried. They tried to be "local," but it never took. To the public, they were still the spoiled kids from the estates and private schools of northwest Chicago, silver spoons still in their mouths. They did some things in such a way, well-meaning notwithstanding, that would make a panhandler throw a $5 handout back in their faces.

Of course, their worst sin was losing. They tried three general managers and six managers and were still losing in the end. They tried to be charitable and recipients asked, "Is that all?"

Strange I should think of this, but fresh in mind is the memory of Paul Richards, deposed, sitting in the Stadium Club at lunch suddenly blurting out, "I don't know the meaning of the word fired. I don't know the meaning of it!"

He'd been fired, but they'd tried to be humane about it and instead they were amputating his pride an inch at a time.

No back door in this arrangement. Ted Turner is now chief operating officer of the Braves, and all he has to do is mail in his monthly payments on time or The Seller will send out and pick up his franchise. The least we can do as he casts off and moves away from the dock is wish him smooth sailing. Bon voyage. And don't take any wooden Indians.

The domineering little man who controlled Augusta National Golf Club and all its affairs announced his choice of a successor, but never called on him to speak. The golfing press stirred nervously during "the kind of moment in which you're not certain if you should laugh or clear your throat," Bisher wrote.

He recalls now: "Cliff Roberts was nice to me, gave me his time and attention, although I was scared to death as I sat there talking to him."

April 8, 1976
The last great autocrat
- - - - -

AUGUSTA, Ga. — It was inevitable that some day we would have to accept that there would no longer be a 77 with Red Grange inside it. Now fat tackles wear it.

That the "Four Horsemen" would eventually become three, then two, then one. That there would be a centerfield in Yankee Stadium without DiMaggio in it. And that Judge Landis would leave baseball a vacant chair.

Nobody really expects Sam Snead to play forever, or A.J. Foyt to race until infinity. Or that Gibraltar will even make it to Doomsday. Even Kelso had to hang it up.

However, the odds were in favor of Clifford Roberts. He wasn't the kind of name you'd find on banners spread across stadium facings. No crowd ever raised a chant in his name, "We want Roberts, we want Roberts!" His face never made bubble gum cards. People never lined up waiting for his autograph — except at the bottom of a check, but somehow or other, our world of the best and the deadline, and the men of high places, fast decision and the thousands who cheer hadn't made proper preparations for the Masters without him.

No more of these news bulletins of propriety and careful rhetoric signed at the bottom, "Clifford Roberts, chairman, Augusta National Golf Club." Nor those Wednesday morning press conferences before the Masters, during which he sat owlishly stern before the flowers of the American press, whose attitude was sometimes as civil as a judge with gout.

This Wednesday he held his last. The man who created America's 51st state used his last one to pronounce himself retired. His years approach 82, and they have worn on him. Monarchs, emperors, czars usually live it out to the end but Clifford Roberts had been looking for a stopping place.

Don't think for one minute that Augusta National Golf Club wasn't — isn't — one of the last of the autocracies. The major reason it survived, grew into the national institution it is through the image of the Masters, is that it was an autocracy. If you get to heaven and find it's run by committees, ask for a transfer.

The power was not self-endowed. In his book, "The Story of Augusta National Golf Club," so fresh off Doubleday's presses even the stores don't have copies yet, Roberts tells of the meeting in January 1933 when Grantland Rice, the sportswriter who was a charter member, stood and made the motion that operation of the club be left entirely in the hands of Bobby Jones and Roberts, and that all meetings be dispensed with.

All members present rose and gave the motion a "rousing aye," he reports, and thus it has been these 43 years. The only commandants this place has ever known have been the two who founded it, and since Jones' death in 1971, Roberts alone.

It's not as if Roberts is turning in his key to the washroom, or catching the next boat to St. Helena. His hand, while not as firm as it once has been, will still be close to the helm. It was the discussion of this unwavering status of his until cutoff date that colored the meet with a tint of comic gravity.

The man who'll succeed him as chairman of the Masters, Bill Lane of Houston, Tex., a fellow of modest physique and a 10 handicap, sat at Roberts' right during the press conference in the main hall of the press building. A head table had been set up on the platform in front of the scoreboard, a little touch of Augusta National transferred to the urgency and the tin-roof clatter of the newsroom down to the spread of a white tablecloth.

"I'm not going to call on him to talk today," Roberts said of Lane, "because I am chairman of this tournament, until its conclusion, and I don't want any interference."

It's the kind of moment in which you're not certain if you should laugh, or clear your throat. Roberts' humor is sometimes drier than an 11-to-1 martini. He meant it, but you also were supposed to laugh.

William H. Lane will be taken care of in other places and other times. He came from Maryville, Tenn., where everybody works for Alcoa, as did his father; went first to Georgia Tech, then to Tennessee after interruption by World War II, and today operates a large food processing conglomerate in Texas. It appears that he has charm, poise, an affable manner and a lot of other savoir faire a fellow acquires after he leaves Maryville, Tenn.

It was the conclusion of a long period of speculation, and of search during which no applications were solicited, and during which nearly every kind of name from a football coach to a "movie star" was introduced.

"At long last I've been fortunate enough to find a successor," Roberts said. "It's no secret that I've been looking for one for a long time. He has arranged his affairs to be able to take on this duty."

"He is the right age, 53. We can expect him to be able to last another 25 years."

And so the transfer of command was as simple as that. Word of it had already leaked out around the grounds. With a committee action, it would have broken in several newspapers and over radio stations days ago. In typical style, when asked whose decision it was, the Last Great Autocrat answered, "Largely mine."

As antiseptic as the change was, and as difficult as it is to involve Roberts in any brush with sentiment, his constant references to "Bob" throughout the announcement and the ensuing exchange with writers crowded along their rows of typewriters belied the fact that beneath the old gentleman's crust there's an element of warm referral to another age that he keeps under close guard.

He may not get sentimental about it, but some of us can, some of the old goats who've been coming here since the age of Truman, and who first arrived as fearfully as we approached our first recital. The fear never departed. It converted itself into respect. For what has taken place here has done more for Augusta, Ga., and golf, than golf has done for any place in the world, with the possible exception of St. Andrews.

In a college football showdown, Herschel Walker of Georgia met George Rogers of South Carolina. The two titans hailed from small towns in Georgia. "In the end... neither settled it," Bisher wrote. "In fact, the strangest kind of twist settled it, and you almost had to be there to understand it."

Nov. 2, 1980
Hercules meets Atlas

- - - - -

ATHENS — They opened proceedings in Sanford Stadium at Saturday noon with the Olympic theme, perfuming the glade in which Georgia's Bulldogs frolic with the fragrance of legend.

Atlas was about to meet Hercules.

Two earth giants would collide, and the nation would watch by the quaint little electronic device that sees all, shows all. Actually, it was a matching of young men and their vast reputes, for their bodies would never touch. They would never be on the field at the same time, for these are not the times of such giants as Grange and Booth.

George Rogers would be matched against Herschel Walker, the senior against the freshman, two men from towns so small their populations combined wouldn't be a good day at Six Flags. In both cases — at South Carolina and Georgia — each is revered as "The Offense," as far as the rest of the nation knows or cares. It would be such a matching of running feet the ground would tremble, and rumblings would rise up beneath us.

We were about to witness an American spectacle. The theme from the Olympic Games was a properly stirring piece of the symphonic to arouse the blood. I know some Frenchman once said that to know America, you must know baseball. To know America in the autumn, my friend, you must know football. You must know college football, as played from Harvard to Humboldt State.

Coming down from the hills Saturday morning, alive with their annual spectacular, the turning of the leaves, it was like a motorcade. They were falling into line from places like Walhalla, Pickens, Liberty and Six-Mile. They came from the big towns with glass skyscrapers. There couldn't be a car left in South Carolina. The Gamecocks haven't known such monumental altitudes since they pumped up their first hog bladder at Columbia. Quiet, old heart, the palpitations are almost too much, and whoever heard of a rooster sweating?

HERSCHEL WALKER

Rogers from Duluth and Walker from Wrightsville, what unlikely addresses for such colossuses, both brought into focus for that glorifying bauble called the Heisman Award. One, Rogers, runs with such terrifying force they call him "animated concrete." The other, Walker, runs from a crouch, as if he's trying to sneak in late at night, and in mesmerizing bursts of speed.

National rankings are as precious as social status in this season of the year, and both teams came here on the prowl for acceptance at the polls. Georgia ranked fourth, South Carolina 14th. It was to be assumed whomever prevailed on these grounds would be beholden to its Rogers or its Walker, and thus he, too, would walk away under the laurel wreath.

Georgia won, 13-10. Walker gained 219 yards, Rogers gained 168. When Walker took out over tackle, searched for the sideline, turned on that after-burning speed and cruised 76 yards for a touchdown after only 46 seconds of the third quarter, it was considered the issue was in hand. Georgia led, 10-0. Walker led Rogers, considerably.

It was then the contest began, and, in the end, it was neither who settled it, one way or the other. In fact, the strangest kind of twist settled it, and you almost had to be here to understand it.

The game had reached the point where Georgia led by only three points. Its defense had seemed to grow quite content with itself, finding itself utterly wealthy, luxuriating on a 13-point lead. South Carolina moved in and kicked a field goal, a (Tim) Rhino holding for a (Eddie) Leopard. Shortly, the Gamecock menagerie was back, and the darnedest thing happened. They gave the ball to a sophomore fullback who had just reached the field, and Carl West, not George Rogers, bolted 39 yards straight down the field for South Carolina's touchdown.

Now we enter the fourth quarter, and Georgia's health is not improving at all. One reason is the kicking game. Mark Malkiewicz had dropped a snap in the first quarter but enterprisingly punted the ball off the ground, soccer style. He hadn't been able to get the hang of it since, and Georgia kept surrendering the ball to South Carolina in lovely position, which is the reason West had only 39 yards to run. That was first down, you see.

Malkiewicz's next punt gave South Carolina the ball on Georgia's 47, and the Gamecocks are pillaging the territory. The Junkyard Dogs, heralded in yore, are tired. It's like watching a dam break with no place to run. Georgia is surely dying in front of 62,000 witnesses when suddenly the good fairy takes over. I said neither Atlas nor Hercules decided it. I was wrong. Rogers, whichever he was, plunged into the line at Georgia's

17-yard area, the ball squirted into the air, Tim Parks, a guard rarely noticed, fell upon it. Saved. But wait.

As the defense had sagged, so had the offense. Or perhaps it was South Carolina's defense. Malkiewicz went back to punt once more, and as in stories of Algerian nature, the downtrodden rise up in the end. The punter was redeemed, though, in the strangest way.

Not only did Malkiewicz get off a boomer, but as he did an unfortunate No. 52, Emanuel Walker by name, crashed into him, not cruelly but 15 yards worth of penalty. Malkiewicz went down in a glorious collapse, Georgia kept the ball. Georgia drove on to South Carolina's one, and Walker achieved his 219th yard. The Gamecocks held gamely there for one last chance. The other end zone was 99 yards away, the clock had 45 seconds to live, South Carolina had the ball, but it was over.

Atlas had defeated Hercules. Or maybe it was the other way around. Take your pick. In Athens, he'll still be known as Herschel. Strike up the Olympic theme one more time for a fadeout, maestro.

Vince Dooley's Bulldogs topped Notre Dame in the Sugar Bowl, capturing the national championship. The Georgia fans "spilled out into the streets, among the taxis and the traffic... wherever two or more Bulldog addicts could get together to embrace, and shriek one more time in deafening unison that mating call of theirs, 'How 'bout them Dawgs!'"

Jan. 2, 1981
Dawgs! Dawgs! Dawgs!
- - - - -

NEW ORLEANS — Luck of the Irish? These people who are watched over by leprechauns? And the good luck fairy? These people who have potatoes and the Arabs have the oil because the Irish had first choice? These people who gave the world Murphy's Law?

You know the definition of Murphy's Law: Anything that can go wrong will go wrong.

Let me tell you about Dooley's Law: Anything that can go right will go right.

Just be patient. Don't press. Just hold your ground and keep your motor running. Be prepared to grasp opportunity by the throat when it arises. Never panic. Even though you may be hanging on the edge of the cliff by your hands and Notre Dame is standing up there stamping on your fingers. Keep cool. Dooley's Law will prevail.

By these measures, by gum and begorra, the University of Georgia Bulldogs are the most celebrated college football team in the nation this day. No. 1 from here to yonder. First 12-0 team in Georgia history, only one in the USA this season, champions of all they behold, including the Southeastern Conference, Clarke County, and now on this monumental occasion, of the Sugar Bowl.

Once they had done in the Irish of Notre Dame, 17-10, the Superdome, the world's largest mushroom, was not large enough to contain the jubilation. The floor of the big parlor was awash with red after it was done. A high-stepping band of young people scheduled to take over after the game were never able to get on the carpet. The howling Dog People wouldn't give it up. This was too big to let go in such a hurry. Some of the players were still milling around among the celebrants long, long afterward. As the clock counted down to 0:00, a red-clad tide gathered along the sideline and then swept out onto the field obliterating the Notre Dame shirts. The Irish seemed to have been swallowed up by this flood of red. Then they began to trickle out of the mob and make a path in their despondency to the locker room.

The celebrants spilled out into the streets, among the taxis and the traffic, along Canal Street, back to the Fairmont Hotel, or wherever two or more Bulldog addicts could get together to embrace, and shriek one more time in deafening unison that mating call of theirs, "HOW 'BOUT THEM DAWGS!"

One more time they forgot and forgave their beloved coach, the Vincent Dooley who had been on the brink of giving them up to return to Auburn, to answer as did that other coach in the state the call of the mother school.

He had seen them through. He had given them the most cherished possession — No. 1. God bless you, St. Vincent, may the light of Heaven forever shine on your sweet head. Lord, how did he ever think he could possibly have lived with them?

Funny thing about this game, it went about like so many other Georgia games have gone this year. The Tennessee game, the Clemson game, the South Carolina game, the Florida game. It was nothing they'll show at the clinics as one of the classics, how football games are to be executed, only how football games are to be won.

A little awkwardly, a little dangerously, a little frustration, a little flirtation with defeat, and then to turn it around and tighten the vise on the victim.

After 16 minutes and 11 seconds Georgia was through scoring. It had its 17 on the board, then spent the rest of the indoor afternoon like a good middleweight fighting off a tough, aggravated heavyweight. They got their points without over-exercising. Say this for the Bulldogs, just crack the door for them, they'll knock it down.

Notre Dame had kicked one field goal and was about to kick another when a kid known only to his family back in Huntsville, Tex., Terry Hoage, busted through and blocked it. Terry Hoage was making his second road trip of the season. He's a freshman, an honor student, a kid who

VINCE DOOLEY

lines up only when the other team kicks. He blocked several for the Scout Squad, the "other" team in practice.

Given the ball at midfield by his block, Georgia converted the break in a 3-3 tie.

Two Notre Dame backs mixed up the second kickoff in a row and Bob Kelly recovered on their one. Herschel Walker scored his first touchdown; 10-3, in 40 seconds.

John Sweeney, a fullback, fumbled, Chris Welton recovered and in three plays Georgia had seven more. Walker ran it in from three yards out in the second minute of the second quarter. You might have sensed a rout, except that Georgia never scored again.

Get this one: The Bulldogs never earned a first down in the second half until the last three minutes. They never completed a pass until the last two minutes.

"But doesn't that tell you something?" said Dooley, a portrait in sweaty ecstacy. "We got it when we really needed it, didn't we, and that's what this team does — it does what it has to when it has to."

Notre Dame was killing them in the second half, but they were hanging on. They still finished the season with fewer first downs, fewer plays and less possession time than their opponents. To show you how it went, Walker led the rushers with 150 yards, but Georgia's net as a team was only 120. Buck Belue was thrown into reverse for more than 50 yards.

By the strangest of coincidences, Dan Devine coached his first bowl team 21 years ago and lost to Georgia in the Orange Bowl when he was at Missouri. Now he has coached in his last — you know, the retirement, and all that — and he loses to Georgia again at Notre Dame.

His record against the great Commonwealth of Georgia this year is something to forget — 0-1-1, to ring up the memory of the tie with Georgia Tech. Oh, a Tech man crashed the Bulldog party for the event. Jimmy Carter and a herd of chums blew in for the game, clogged traffic for several minutes before the kickoff, then visited the Georgia locker room afterwards, à la Richard M. Nixon. Presumably he didn't design the second-half offense.

Celebrants were still noising up the night past the witching hour. New Year's Eve got a 24-hour extension. Bulldog red was scattered about from Metairie to Algiers. No Real Certified Georgia Bulldog ever reveled in such a paradise. In 1942 they were No. 2, in 1946 they were No. 3, but there's nothing like No. 1. And if you don't believe it just look up.

Some of the Dawgs are flying so high they won't be able to hit ground until next week or find Athens again until next year.

No sports team had caused Bisher, or his readers, more frustration over the years than the Atlanta Falcons. At last in 1980 they had won a divisional title and, as their fans whooped and hollered, led the wild-card Dallas Cowboys by 14 points going into the fourth quarter. But then, as Bisher wrote, "everything came crashing down" on Atlanta's often-forlorn NFL team.

Jan. 5, 1981
The real America's Team

- - - - -

Fetch me my house slippers, the comfy ones with the fur lining. Turn off the TV and turn up the gentle music, just let me sit here and muse.

It's over. Like a short, sweet romance it came to a crashing end. It was like a sad movie in which the heroine dies, the lights come up and you walk out into the daylight and life goes on.

At least you can say you had a taste of the wine. You romped with the nymphs. They led you deep into the forest, but you lost your way. You were almost beginning to think you were America's team there for awhile, weren't you?

It is better to have loved and lost than never to have loved at all, they say. The hell it is. And who are "they" anyway?

The Falcons were closer than close. They were 15 minutes away from going further than any Falcons have gone since creation. They were leading the Dallas Cowboys by 14 points. They had led by 10, and would lead by 10 again. They had it in their satchel. Then they began playing like a golfer leading the U.S. Open, trying not to make a bogey, and they made a card full of bogeys.

It was almost like somebody up there was saying, "Look, guys, have your fun. You can come close, but don't forget. Dallas wins. After all, they're... well, they're Dallas."

This was another peg up in the Falcons' social climb. The Cowboys had to come to THEM. THEY were the champs. The game was on their grass, not at that place in Texas with the hole in the roof.

But who were these upstarts, anyway? These social climbers. How many Super Bowls had they been to, these guys who were toddling

STEVE BARTKOWSKI

around their mama's knee, driving a second-hand Mustang with a raccoon tail on the aerial, the old radio playing big rock, trying all the cures for acne, while the Cowboys were endearing themselves to America. Them with the big blue stars on the hats. While Roger Staubach was coming back from the Navy, leading them onward and outward — from Dallas to suburban Irving.

How dare these whippersnappers lead the Dallas Cowboys in the fourth quarter! It was almost as if they had something of the same feeling. What are people going to say about this? Run, clock, run!

Dallas scores another touchdown. It's 24-17. But the Falcons get three back on a field goal. It's 10 again. That old safe feeling comes back.

Here come the Cowboys again, five passes, 62 yards, two minutes, 57 seconds, touchdown. If you've ever had tonsilitis, you know how the throats were feeling.

Once the Falcons were a team built on a foundation of defense. Now there was a switch. The offense could save the defense. Just get two first downs, two measly pieces of ground 10 yards wide in three plays each, kick the ball and leave "America's Team" nothing but their shirttails. The clock would be down to seconds.

Three plays make three yards. Punt. In a minute and six seconds the Cowboys are back in the end zone again. Everything comes crashing down. You know, that old un-towering feeling, not exactly as in the song?

I never did like that three-man rush, anyway. It'll get you and your secondary both killed. Danny White, vice-quarterback to Staubach so many seasons, was having his own way. The first half he passed for only 83 yards, mainly because the Falcons had the ball so much. By the end he was up to 322. He had enough time to call his broker while his catchers scattered. Give a good QB that long, he'll complete passes and he'll beat you. The three guys up front were like three guys trying to break into a bank vault with a Boy Scout knife.

All the Cowboys were trying to do was get into field goal range, tie it and have a shot at overtime. Danny White said it after it was over. It reminded you of the earlier Falcons of the season. Just hang in there and sometimes good will happen. This time the Falcons were the "other guys."

It is not as if they didn't have their high moments. Alfred Jenkins made a catch on the way to the third touchdown that ought to be engraved. He was under double coverage. Rep. Pridemore, chairman of the secondary, struck again and once plucked off a pass that set up the last three points, and another time picked up a fumble when Dallas was on the threshhold of another score. He almost did a Roy Riegels on it, took a step in the wrong direction before he caught himself. Steve Bartkowski put in another honorable performance, considering that his running game was pretty well shut down.

Down by the third base dugout a bunch of flesh was being revealed during the second half by some guys dressed only in their skin from the waist up. All about them were residents bundled in parkas and fur in the chilled twilight. This spontaneous convening of an improvised "Polar Bare Club" was sweaty in its enthusiasm for the moment. They waved a Falcons flag. They whooped in delight. They envisioned a visit next Sunday by the Philadelphia Eagles, to be followed by another glorious Georgia march on New Orleans.

In 10 minutes, the flag was down. Shirts were back on. Goose pimples had replaced the sweat beads. Chins were at half-mast. Life had taken a sudden crash around them. "Well, we came close," a hardy consoler said, walking down the exit ramp.

The adjacent reply will not be published here this week.

Bitsy Grant was the mighty mite of U.S. tennis. The sports legend once was Bisher's insurance agent. In their last conversation, Grant lamented the theft of a dog and the car the dog was sitting in. "All Bitsy wanted back was his pooch," Bisher wrote. "The hell with the car. That was Bitsy loyalty for you."

June 6, 1986
A 125-pound package of grit

- - - - -

Bryan M. Grant Jr. was only a name on a marker by the side of Northside Drive to thousands who passed on the way to work each day. All they knew was that it announced the proximity of some tennis courts. Not many knew whether there was a Bryan M. Grant Jr. — probably the precinct councilman — and fewer still realized that the one and the same might be out there playing his game.

Rare is the athlete, no matter how celebrated, who has been privileged to play on grounds bearing his own name. Old Atlanta was pretty thoughtful about ennobling its own. Right next door is the Bobby Jones Golf Course, a glorious name squandered on a trifling municipal project. If it ever fell Jones' misfortune to play a round on it, it escaped me.

Bryan M. Grant Jr. was "Bitsy" for the reason that there wasn't much of him. He was so small that his father, quite a player himself, passed him over and dwelt upon trying to make the bigtime player out of his bigger brother, Berry. It was left to Mama, if the runt of the litter was to get any training, and so we score another victory for the lady of the house.

Bitsy was impossibly undersized for international tennis, a destroyer among battleships, a Volkswagen against Packards. If any athlete ever inspired the word "competitor," it was this 125-pound package of grit. He took on Donald Budge, who was tall and strong. He took on

Ellsworth Vines, who was tall and had the wingspan of a bomber. Each was the finest player in the world in his prime. It is duly recorded in the history of tennis that Bitsy Grant laid upon them the worst defeat of their careers, Vines at Forest Hills in 1933, Budge in Miami in 1937.

BITSY GRANT

Bitsy had a way of leaving a big hurt on some big men. I'd guess the high moment of his long career, fought as a bantamweight among Goliaths, was the Davis Cup matches of 1937. He had been bypassed for the U.S. team so many times the South had worked up a strong hate toward the stiffbacks who ran the USLTA. There was one man up there who liked him, Walter Pate, Davis Cup captain that year. Against the better judgment of all, Pate appointed Grant as Budge's singles partner against the Australians in a challenge match.

He knocked off Jack Bromwich one day and Jack Crawford the next, at a time when the Aussies were two of the finest players in the world. As smashing as it was, when it came to picking the team to play the British in the finals, Bitsy was put down again and Atlanta bared its saber.

When it was all summed up, though, the day he beat Vines, such a versatile fellow that he later became a winning player on the golf tour, was the day of deepest satisfaction.

"That was my greatest thrill in tennis," he said some years ago. He had beaten Vines on grass. Dirt was his surface, good old Georgia red dirt upon which Mama had taught him.

"That wasn't the best I ever played on grass, though. That was when I beat von Cramm at Forest Hills in 1937."

That match ran out to five sets and into the darkness, "brilliantly and fiercely fought," as was written in those days. Bitsy had to win the last two sets to beat the German baron, upon which the West Side Tennis Club erupted into a frenzied ovation.

Bitsy led the nation in retiring, and as many times as he retired, he unretired. The doggedness in him wouldn't let him quit. Small as he was, he even tried basketball at North Carolina and made the freshman team. It was there that he came upon his doubles partner of long years standing, Wilmer Hines, a South Carolinian later followed by Russell Bobbitt, an Atlanta comrade.

Those were the days of long white ducks, tournaments at the club, and restrictive behavior. John McEnroe would have been sent to the woodshed. Bitsy lived close enough to censure. He had a temper as large as his body was small. He could scorch a pasture with his venom, but usually his severe remarks were addressed to himself, not some courtly gentleman in the chair.

He was my insurance consultant for years, meticulously dealing with the most insignificant item. He spoke with a nervous delivery and punctuated conversation with a matching laugh. Rarely did he ever speak of the game. Yet, it was his life to the point that as recent as two months ago he was still on the court at the center they named for him.

The last time we talked, he called about a stolen dog. Some thief had purloined his car and inside the car, which Bitsy had left running to keep his animal cool on a hot summer's day, was his beloved pet. The car had been stolen, too, but all Bitsy wanted back was his pooch. The hell with the car.

That was Bitsy loyalty for you, the wee fellow who died yesterday of cancer. Strangely, you might say, the big brother Berry died just a few weeks ago in Charlotte. Both cut down by the same killer.

His first load of laundry sent home from college came back washed, and with a batch of cookies. That was just one of the tender memories of a loving mother. At her death, Bisher profiled her for his readers because, he wrote, "you have the right to know something more about what lies behind that cragginess that peers out at you daily from the top of this pillar of piffle."

Dec. 31, 1986
No longer will it be home

- - - - -

DENTON, N.C. — Standing on the curb looking down upon the flickering lights of the modest business center of my hometown, the municipal Christmas ornaments still in place, it finally descended upon me, the desolate feeling that after all these years I must now face life without a parent.

Behind me, in the funeral parlor, the lighting reverently dimmed, the well-meant conversation, from which I had escaped, reverently hushed, lay my mother free of pain at last. Ninety-four years seemed such a short time now.

"The end of an era in this town," the minister said in his eulogy.

He was a young man whose straightforward sermonics had pleased my mother when he served the Denton charge. Such Godliness in youth appealed to her, and she wanted no ancient orator intoning over her last rites.

"As close to a saint as I shall ever know," one of her adoring grandsons had said.

I hasten to declare her free of old-revival stodginess. She was of hearty spirit, she could laugh, listen well, resist with quiet stubbornness, enjoyed eating, and her kitchen was famed in its province.

Testimonial to that was an embroidered verse framed on the wall: "No matter where I serve my guests, It seems they like my kitchen best," it read.

Just a month ago I walked into her room and she was upright in bed crocheting an afghan one of her granddaughters had been working on for a year.

"I told Ann she was never going to finish that thing," she said, "bring it to me and I'd finish it for her."

MAMIE BISHER

She did. Just in time.

She was sick in bed the day my dad drove me off to college. When I sent my first batch of laundry home, she returned it with some of her cookies. I was reassured.

When I called and asked to switch from Furman to North Carolina, when I discovered journalism had been dropped at Furman, there was never a pause, though I had finally reached a scholarship state which eased the financial pain. Journalism was as foreign to them as Tibet. There wasn't even a newspaper in town. They felt confident enough that their guidance was worth a further investment of their faith.

For all the wrath that I have directed at television, it was the magic eye that nurtured her belated interest in sports. The tube brought her Atlantic Coast Conference basketball, and could rile her or pleasure her. Jim Thacker, the broadcaster, several times volunteered to drop by and escort her to a game, but she felt she'd be a burden. Her devotion centered on N.C. State, the Wolfpack. Her brother had been superintendent of the physical plant at State for over three decades, and a building on the campus is named for him. She thought this was worthy of partiality.

Besides, "I don't like the way Dean Smith acts at the games. Is he ever happy?" When she did finally break into the bigtime as a spectator, it was at the top. She came to Atlanta for the Final Four in 1978, and those were the only games she ever saw in person. She went home content to leave it to TV, and gloried in it when N.C. State startled the world at Albuquerque. Someone even prevailed upon Jim Valvano to send her a note. Frankly, she wasn't greatly impressed.

She would have rankled at being identified in death as "Mamie M. Bisher." Let the moderns go in their own style, if they please. She was "Mrs. C. Bisher" in her eyes. Her life was her man. Family and church came in where they fit in, but always in the photo.

Forgive me, if I have intruded on your good nature with something so heavily personal. But my heart is heavy. My loss is great. The hurt runs deep. Somehow, no matter how prepared I thought I was, I came up short.

Beyond that, those of you who care have the right to know something more about what lies behind that cragginess that peers out at you daily from the top of this pillar of piffle. The important things. To know that whatever may have gone wrong with this creature could not be traced to the hearth.

It was the morning of Dec. 30, 1986, 8 o'clock, a layer of frost coating the brown leaves, that I drove out of the yard for the last time. No longer will it ever be home again. Without parent, without mother, home is no more.

Bisher and the National Basketball Association have never made a perfect match, even during the late 1980s when there were stirring battles between the Atlanta Hawks, then coached by Mike Fratello, and the Detroit Pistons. "Some time I wish I could come away from a professional basketball game not feeling like I've been to a human demolition derby," the columnist writes.

May 6, 1987
Hockey without pads

- - - - -

Well, Atlanta's back in love again. The Hawks lost a game Sunday. By a point. There was great mourning and gnashing of the gums and resignation.

They won one Tuesday night. Now everybody wants to take them home to dinner or bake them a cake.

Me, some time I wish I could come away from a professional basketball game not feeling like I've been to a human demolition derby. When the Hawks play the Detroit Pistons you don't expect a lot of manners. There won't be a lot of bowing and scraping and, "After you, Isiah," or "Dreadfully sorry, Mr. Laimbeer."

It's more like ice hockey without pads and sticks. One thing you can count on in a basketball game, no fight is going to last long. A basketball player throws a punch only after great deliberation. Nearly everything he has is exposed.

There were minor frays during the evening at The Omni, where they love to hate Bill Laimbeer. Once he and Cliff Levingston came wrestling down the court like two drunks trying to hold one another up. The whistle blew and the call was one you don't see often in the NBA, a double foul.

Once it was over and all parties had been safely delivered to their assigned boudoirs, the most serious casualty was a coach. Mike Fratello was deeply wounded, and nobody had laid a glove on him.

Sunday afternoon the Hawks had opened the second round of the playoff on their own boards, and though they had not played with brilliance, they had lost by only a point. Their coach had awakened Monday to the sounds of doom by air and the sight of it in the printed word.

"We just lost one game, by one point, and the people out there are selling this team down the river," Mike said, his face etched in pain.

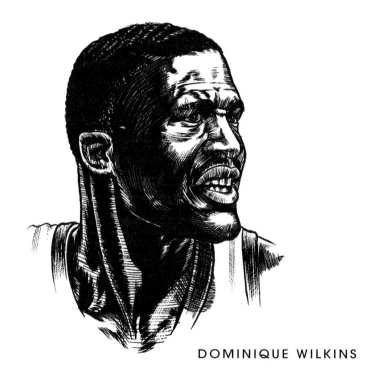

DOMINIQUE WILKINS

"Doesn't anybody ever give these young men any credit? This is a great team they were playing. You'd have thought the bottom had dropped out. ONE point!"

This time it was 13 on the right side, 115-102. The Hawks had blown out the Pistons at the start, slumped into their old rut, scratching, clawing, trying to find something that had gotten away. Each time when they cried out for help during the evening, they found it in the same place, a dark-haired, implacable object wearing No. 10.

Randy Scott Wittman, apparently named for the old movie sheriff himself, was in pain before it began, a back problem. He had an appointment with a chiropractor, but the chiropractor was having enough trouble trying to stay alive himself. A sudden case of meningitis.

So Wittman came to the arena untreated. Some of us have to make sacrifices. Some of us have to play hurting. What he did was twist and fake and bump and run and give the Hawks some substitute offense while the Pistons kept Dominique Wilkins under double, and sometimes triple surveillance. When the big gun is in the throes of the trap, you want to get the ball to the other side of the court, for somebody has to be over there, and often it was Wittman.

The Hawks' first two baskets were made on feeds by Wittman, then the Indiana gunner went to work himself. "Wittman 17-foot jumper. Wittman 9-foot jumper. Wittman 13-foot jumper. Wittman 19-foot jumper."

When all the bodies had been accounted for, Wittman had hit on 15 of 25 shots from the floor for 34 points. While the Pistons had lavished much attention on Wilkins, figuring you stop Wilkins, you stop the Hawks, Wittman had feasted on his freedom.

"I was fired up," he said. That was easy to see. "Just knowing we had to have this game so much."

Wittman was a glittering star at Indiana, co-player of the year in the Big Ten, scoring leader and All-American, which isn't too bad for a slow white kid who can't leap, an inhumane description that travels with him like part of his name. His contribution to the Hawks is wreathed in selflessness as much as points.

There was great concern among the full house of patrons that this matching might turn into a street brawl. The patrons had arrived pledged to vent their venom on Laimbeer, a Notre Dame grad whose major offense is his ponderosity. He's built like an 18-wheeler, and plays like one, but has the delicate shooting touch of a Maserati.

Rick Mahorn has developed into a pretty good scorer for a hatchet man. Isiah Thomas performs with a gloating, floats about, occasionally touching the floor, effecting this impish innocence. Dennis Rodman is one of the league's hot dogs. Vinnie Johnson comes off the bench looking like No-Neck Williams and shooting the lights out.

John Salley was grief-stricken that he had been booed at The Omni. "Booed, here in Atlanta, my town," he said.

He has become more a force in the NBA than the most optimistic had expected. What he fails to realize is that when he took off the Gold and White of Georgia Tech and came to work in the Piston blue, he became the enemy. Such are the travails of the mercenary.

Now they turn and make for the suburbs of Detroit, where this war in skivvies will continue. That's the way all wars should be fought anyway, half in one country, half in the other, so the devastation can be spread around.

In his fortieth year as lead sports columnist of The Journal, *Bisher sent this deadline report from Tokyo for The* Journal's *historic front page when Atlanta was awarded the Olympic Games. "This was happening at night in Tokyo, and I had to get to the typewriter. I had an hour to make the first edition," he recalls. Atlanta was selected over Athens, Greece, a favorite in some circles. "The race has been run," Bisher wrote, "and the tortoise beat the hare again."*

Sept. 18, 1990
The tortoise again beats the hare

- - - - -

TOKYO — You'd probably better take this sitting down. Find a chair.

Take a cold drink of water. Brace yourself. Clear your head.

Citius, altius, fortius, Atlantius.

You have just become the parents of the Olympic Games. Not just any old Olympic games, but the 100th birthday Games. The 1996 Olympic Games, the centennial year of rebirth.

Senor Juan Antonio Samaranch, president of the International Olympic Committee, took his stance at the podium before a packed auditorium in the New Takanawa Prince Hotel, and a worldwide television audience, Tuesday night about 8:45 (Tokyo time) and let the world hear the news.

The IOC had made its choice. Not Athens, the most feared rival, for it was there the Games were revived in 1896; not Melbourne, the Australian city considered the best compromise choice; not Toronto, Atlanta's North American rival; not Manchester, England; not Belgrade, Yugoslavia; but ATLANTA, county seat of Fulton, capital of the state of Georgia. After four ballots, it boiled down to Atlanta and Athens — the one in Greece, not the one in Clarke County — and

Atlanta took the Greek capital on the fifth ballot, 51-35.

So once again it was proved that it ain't over till it's over, and in this case, until 86 fat ladies sang. Eighty-seven delegates were advertised, but one was missing for reasons unknown by this correspondent.

It has been a long, hard climb from zero to the top of the mountain for Billy Payne, the attorney and former Georgia football player who came up with this crazy idea and quarterbacked it from embryo to success.

BILLY PAYNE

Final presentations had been made during the day, Atlanta leading off, and Payne verging on tears in his emotional pitch.

He probably cried again after the announcement, but you couldn't tell from where I sat. Atlantans, here in droves, leaped to their feet, shrieking. So did several other portions of the building, but a stunned silence fell over the European and Australian delegations.

From Georgia, there were two governors; two mayors; an all-star cast of Atlanta's business giants; the president of Georgia Tech, Pat Crecine; and even Vince Dooley, athletics director of Georgia, among the celebrants.

"Coca-Cola!" someone cried out in the peanut gallery of the section where I sat. Sure enough, the Coca-Cola people were outside, distributing Atlanta '96 Olympic pins. Throughout, though, Coca-Cola, which does 80 percent of its business outside the United States, has firmly maintained its neutrality.

Atlanta has pounded on its breast for several years, proclaiming itself "the world's next great city." If it was or wasn't, this is one major brick in its foundation. It was Lord Kilannin (Hugh Morris), the Irishman, who said "80 percent of the delegates come here with their mind made up." If that be so, that speaks volumes for the forthright, rather than clever, the down-home, rather than sophisticated campaign the Atlantans carried out, even to the Tokyo scene.

After making their in-person presentation Tuesday morning, Payne said that "we did everything we could. We can only hope it's enough." It was like a surgeon who pronounces the operation a success, but whether the patient lives or dies, you find out later.

The Games had played in Los Angeles in 1984, and this was considered Atlanta's most serious drawback. "We tried to move Atlanta as far from Los Angeles as possible," he said.

It is possible that the Greeks shot themselves in the foot with their possessive approach, their brashness, their aggressiveness to the point of hauling in three Americans of Greek heritage to speak for them.

When they ran a two-page spread in the *Japan Times* Monday, that caused considerable disbelief. If that wasn't enough, then their press conference Tuesday morning may have been the final stroke.

"We didn't come here to give you minutes of the meeting," Prime Minister Constantine Mitsotakis said.

In the hallway outside the interview room, the mayor of Athens and a member of the press got into a fist fight. Later, the Greek delegation called a second press conference to apologize for the first.

Maybe the damage had been done. Maybe there was no damage at all.

Maybe it was Atlanta all the way, but, no, that can't be true. Athens led on the first two votes and Atlanta got into the race only on the third, a 26-26 tie with Athens.

Well, the party's not over. It's just beginning. The game has been played, and played well. The race has been run, and the tortoise beat the hare again.

The Bisher pen can be unsparing, and his columns rarely personal. However, each year a truce is declared, and personal insights become plentiful, as he writes his annual Thanksgiving column. It is one of the most eagerly awaited Bisher columns for Atlanta readers.

Nov. 22, 1990
Time to be thankful

- - - - -

Ah, yes, Thanksgiving time. That holiday set aside for us to be grateful for all the good things in life. And for me, a time to line them up item by item, some in folly, some in cynicism, some in loving admiration, all mixed up together like a tossed salad:

I'm thankful for the backroads that take you through small towns and away from the speed demons and the roar of interstates.

I'm thankful for the waitress who can smile and makes you glad you're at her table.

I'm thankful for fried catfish.

I'm thankful for the 6-foot basketball player, because he has to be an athlete.

I'm thankful for a new shirt, but why do they have to load them with all those wicked pins? I'm thankful for my kind of race horse, one that wins with my bucks on his nose.

I'm thankful when I see a funeral procession pass, and it's not mine.

I'm thankful for a little island off Scotland known as Islay. (You say it "Eye-lay.") I'm thankful for old, comfortable clothes. (I don't care how they look. I'm not modeling.) I'm thankful for George Foreman, otherwise we'd have had no Senior Citizens heavyweight title division.

I'm thankful for Monday Night Football — on radio. (No bedsheet messages, no three hours of Three Stooges repartee.) I'm thankful for Jim Koger, who gave up sports broadcasting and turned his life to something humanitarian. (It's El Shaddai Mission in Columbus, where he and wife Joanne, and others, look out for the cares and needs of the less blessed.) I'm thankful for grits, if I don't have to eat them (it?).

I'm thankful for the sound of Santa Claus's ho, ho ho, even if he is a big, old fraud.

I'm thankful for those among us who realize that afternoon newspapering ain't dead.

I'm thankful for Cypress Point, Butler National and all those other clubs that exercise their right to privacy and to bathe and powder down without fear of female invasion.

I'm thankful for the football player who scores a touchdown, then politely hands the football to an official.

I'm thankful for the NBA, though for the life of me I can't think why.

I'm thankful for those three pairs of little bronzed shoes on my desk at home, and Lord, how I wish the feet were small and back in those shoes again.

I'm thankful for the memory of the mesmerizing fragrance of my mother's kitchen during holidays.

I'm thankful the Scottish Rite Game has re-established itself on Thanksgiving Day, for that is where it belongs.

I'm thankful I don't dip snuff.

I'm thankful for all those guys who've come to call themselves "the Bisher Boys." (Might as well be, since Lewis Grizzard has opened up all our secrets, including what a terror I was to work for. And he is right. I was anything but easy.)

I'm thankful I still have a place to Be Thankful each year.

The Rambling Wrecks dismantled powerful Nebraska to win a national championship of college football for the first time since 1952. It was decisive. "Georgia Tech had husked Nebraska's corn," Bisher wrote. "'Big Red' had been bleached to a light shade of pink."

Jan. 2, 1991
A wave of Techmania

- - - - -

ORLANDO — It would be another day before anything would be official, and 800 million Chinese and 25 million Siberians didn't give a damn, anyway. In the Citrus Bowl in Orlando, on the shore of lovely Lake Lorna Doone, however, Techmania had broken out, '90s style.

Out of the stands came a flood of the color gold, and soon the playing surface, where the war of Georgia Tech vs. Nebraska had just been fought, was a seething sea of it. The highly intelligent message board spelled out the words: "Georgia Tech 1990 National Champions."

A bit presumptuous, perhaps, for the final results were yet to be heard from the County of Dade. It would come later in the evening, but for the nonce, in the heart of every Georgia Tech Yellow Jacket, there was only one verdict to be rendered: Georgia Tech, the only unbeaten major team in the country, America's football champion.

So they celebrated. At 5:15 p.m., one goal post came down. A cordon of guards had congealed under the other and stood their ground until they remembered the wife and kids at home, facing the mass that moved in one flowing wave, and at 5:20, the other came down. A few heads were bloodied, some blows were struck, but in the end, the supporters of the Old Gold and White proved they can be as destructive as the worst.

Georgia Tech had not beaten Nebraska, Georgia Tech had husked Nebraska's corn. "Big Red" had been bleached to a light shade of pink. It was not a rout. Georgia Tech's defense, once a very dear asset, had seen to that. That marvelous secondary seemed to take a nap with a 21-0 lead, and it's quite probable that Ken Swilling postponed his professional debut for a year, unintentionally. A couple of times, the heralded

BOBBY ROSS

safety was plucked as clean as a supermarket fryer.

What no Georgia Tech team had done since the great champions of 1952, Georgia Tech '90 had done. What no coach had been able to do since Bobby Dodd, the legend, Bobby Ross, who would rather be right than legendary, had done 38 years later. His team had survived the rapids of an unbeaten season.

What no Georgia Tech team had ever done, this Georgia Tech team did. This team scored 45 points in a bowl game, a record, for what that's worth. The team of 1954 scored 42 points against West Virginia in the

Sugar Bowl.

But so much for the mundane, for statistics that can only address the era in which they are posted. Madness breaks out in such noble moments as these, and it was impossible that they should be able to choke back the inevitable chant being held captive in their throats.

"We're Number One! We're Number One! We're Number One!" they cried.

If the balloteers who decide in this most imprecise electoral college were not yet committed, this was the campaign cry to get their attention. They — the voters — are mere mortal sportswriters and broadcasters. This was the voice of Georgia Tech speaking in behalf of the only unbeaten football team in the upper crust.

It had been convincing from the outset. Check this drive: Georgia Tech takes the opening kickoff. Seventy yards, nine plays and three minutes, 15 seconds later, Georgia Tech is leading 7-0. Biggest of the plays was also the most comedic. Shawn Jones, the slippery quarterback, found his foot in the grasping hand of a linebacker named Dan Svehla, was going down, it seemed, than yanked the foot free and did go down, but 46 yards later.

Check this one: Jones hits Greg Lester for 38 yards, then William Bell takes care of the rest of a 64-yard drive in three plays, sprawling into the end zone.

And this one: Three plays, 71 yards, the final 57 that kid Bell again, briefly clogged up in the middle, then breaking loose, again diving into the end zone exhausted. The Jerry Mays who could never be replaced, has been, even more gloriously.

The final score, 45-21, is a big one even against Swarthmore. But this was Nebraska, mighty Nebraska, of the mighty and haughty Big Eight, whose other candidate member for No. 1, Colorado, would be making its final campaign appeal in the Orange Bowl against Notre Dame.

No matter what, strains of "Rambling Wreck" were ringing out in hoarse disharmony in bars, taverns and eateries of Orlando World, and wherever as many as two Yellow Jackets got together Tuesday night. Only a few years ago they had to come to grips with the message that Georgia Tech might become the Carnegie Tech of the South and play in a swell little fraternal conference with Centre, Washington & Lee and Hampden-Sydney. Now the Jackets were restored to the glory of a day long gone and muchly cherished.

The wonder was if Tom Osborne could go home to Nebraska again after this — 45 points to Oklahoma, 45 points to Georgia Tech. And the 21 Nebraska had scored here were put up by a quarterback who had never thrown a touchdown pass before. Tom Haase is the name.

Meanwhile, they hoisted Bobby Ross's little body to their massive shoulders, Mike Mooney for one, and lugged him to the center of the field, there to be met by the man his team had humbled. He had known that dismal feeling. He had wondered if it would ever change at Georgia Tech.

If the coach he was supposed to be would ever be the coach he could be again.

Now, he knows. Great reward comes to the man blessed with the virtue of patience.

In one of the miracles of sport, the Atlanta Braves, owned by Ted Turner, went from last in a division to first in the National League. "The frog turned into a prince," Bisher writes. "The nightmare turned into a dream. Ted Turner not only knows the thrill of a pennant, he knows what the infield fly rule is."

Oct. 18, 1990
From worst to first

- - - - -

PITTSBURGH — There he stood, wearing a striped shirt and striped tie, the same Ted Turner who had stood before a dinner audience 15 years ago and promised Atlanta a World Series before he even knew what a passed ball or a pennant was. He thought pennants were as easily won as an America's Cup. Winning came easy to him.

Instead, Robert Edward Turner gave Atlanta 14 years of defeat, except for one short interruption of happiness, as deceiving as St. Elmo's fire. "America's Team" became America's Joke, famed on cable from coast to coast, but mainly as doormat of the National League.

Well, put all that behind you now. The warts are gone. The frog turned into a prince. The nightmare turned into a dream. Ted Turner not only knows the thrill of a pennant, he knows what the infield fly rule is.

A pennant! A date with a World Series! Title it, "Fifteen Years from Purchase to Pennant."

The Atlanta Braves have had Twins, or will have.

The theme was pitching. Pitching. Pitching. Pitching. Three shutouts and an earned-run average of 1.57, quite necessary since the mighty bats went into a sudden coma, except for one 10-run spasm on the home ground.

Three kids named Glavine, Avery and Smoltz, young, talented, mature beyond their years and unimpressed with themselves. And the last of these was Smoltz, John Andrew Smoltz, right-handed, who twice delivered the precious moment, first the division championship, now the pennant.

JOHN SCHUERHOLZ

On Aug. 12, 1987, the Braves traded a crochety veteran, Doyle Alexander, to the Detroit Tigers for a yearling named Smoltz. His earned-run average was a plump 5.58 and his record was 4-and-10, not as a Tiger, but with the Glens Falls farm club in New York. The Tigers were looking for an old arm down the stretch in the pennant race.

Alexander produced, but still the Tigers didn't make it. Just the other day, Sparky Anderson, the Tigers manager, mourned the deal that cost him the kid who was known as "the best arm in the league at Glens

Falls." With Smoltz, the Tigers might have been there this year. They weren't, but Smoltz, with the delivery of his six-hit shutout, which Brian Hunter ended on one hop off the bat of Jose Lind, accomplished the feat for Atlanta — from worst in the major leagues to best in the National, with more to come.

"It's incredible," manager Bobby Cox said, "two shutouts when we were two games down, and in the Pirates' own park."

The last time Pittsburgh scored a run was 22 innings and three days ago in Atlanta. If ever you saw a ballclub that looked beat from the first pitch, it was the Pirates. Pittsburgh, the city, must have felt it. The only suspense of the night was waiting for the attendance to be announced — 46,932. Ten thousand seats were unsold, for some peculiar reason. Even the Goodyear blimp didn't show up.

When the Braves struck quickly in the first, featuring rookie Hunter's two-run homer that hugged the foul pole, the Pirates went quietly. Their malady could be traced to the center of power that got them here, the "Killer Bs" and Andy Van Slyke. Combined, Van Slyke, Bobby Bonilla and Barry Bonds campaigned for most valuable player in the league, hit an even .200. Combined, they were 2-for-12 against Smoltz.

Who can even remember as far ago as the spring, when the Braves were breaking in a new infield, the gift of free agency, if you can look at a price of $17 million or more and call it a gift. John Schuerholz, the new general manager from Kansas City, had presented Cox with Terry Pendleton for third base, Sid Bream for first and Rafael Belliard for shortstop.

They were almost as far behind on the Fourth of July as the "Miracle Braves" of 1914. They were the first Braves champions, but this is just as much a miracle, if not more. Those Braves had come from fifth to first, these from last to first.

It wasn't a stroll through a meadow for Smoltz right off. Van Slyke hit humongous shots his first two at-bats that would have won the long-drive contest. But as the game wore on — which it did for 189 minutes — they paraded to the plate, Jay Bell, the Pirates' leading hitter, Van Slyke, Bonilla and Bonds, and went down like the soldiers at Gallipoli.

Try as hard as it might, all those big-screen inspirationals, as weird, goofy and cockeyed as they are at Three Rivers, could barely raise a whoopee in Pittsburghers' throats.

Once again, in the eighth inning, the city's police cavalry and special squadsmen came onto the field, four horses each transforming each bullpen into a horsepen. They would not be needed. Only those assigned to escort Turner and party from seats behind the Braves' dugout to the clubhouse had a special mission to carry out.

The scene there conformed to custom. Much champagne was wasted, some consumed. Players cheerfully sprayed each other with the juice of the grape, and it was there that Turner came into possession of the bulky trophy, presented by President Bill White, a former first baseman.

There wasn't much left to say. This was the dream realized, a dream 26 years old now, time for kids to be born, grow up, go to college and get a job. Twenty-six years from the day Tony Cloninger threw the first pitch in Atlanta Stadium, and the Atlanta Braves broke into major league life losing their first game to — who else? — the Pittsburgh Pirates.

Of all the sports, golf is tops, and of all the venues, Augusta National Golf Club ranks first with Bisher. "There is no more attractive setting for any sports event in the world."

April 5, 1992
Meet me at Yellow Jasmine

- - - - -

Hardly a week passes but what somebody will ask, "What's your favorite sports event?" And when it comes out The Masters, they say, "What makes it so great, especially when hardly anybody can get a ticket?" Not only that, but why is it so great to a journalist who has to cover it outside the ropes like any common, ordinary unwashed spectator? We'll get around to that later.

First reason for The Masters is that it's a living memorial to Robert T. Jones Jr. Some skeptics said it would never survive Jones's death. But it has. Then it would never survive Clifford Roberts's death.

But it has.

One of the most misunderstood but most innovative men in sport was Clifford Roberts. The Masters was his idea. Jones was the lure in the partnership. Roberts appeared gruff and unapproachable, but he had good ears, he solicited suggestions and never made any move fractiously. Jones was the model sportsman. His pursuit of the game ended when there were no more jousts to be jousted. Money was not his goal, because there was little of it to be won, and besides, he played as an amateur. He retired at the age of 28.

The standards established by Jones and Roberts have varied little.

One year, in a weather bind, the field was allowed to tee off on the first and 10th holes at the same time, a dreadful crime never since repeated.

The Jones-Roberts rules of order have survived two succeeding chairmen, Bill Lane and Hord Hardin, and will be zealously upheld by the third, newly chosen, Jackson Stephens, an Arkansas tycoon, which is the same in Arkansas as anyplace else.

The membership has maintained its strongly elite level, no invasion by maverick elements. Thus, the preservation of all the original standards and high principle. Raucousness is not tolerated. Spectators with any doubt as to how to comport themselves have the original pamphlet composed by Robert T. Jones Jr. himself to refer to.

There is no more attractive setting for any sports event in the world than Augusta National Golf Club. It is not by accident, but long and concentrated planning.

The grounds are not a clutter of corporate tents hustling clients with booze and food, encouraging golf not to be watched, though the majority of members are corporate men. Members once were resentful when Roberts insisted they wear distinguishable garb and be available to help spectators who had questions. "They said they felt like hotel bellmen," he said. Now they can't wait to get into their green jackets when they reach the tournament.

The Masters maintains reasonable rates at its concession stands, staffed by personable young people from the Augusta area. Satisfying one's appetite or thirst is not a major investment. Most expensive sandwich costs $2 — the delicious pimiento cheese is only a buck — Coca-Cola 75 cents, beer $1.50, and candy bars and other such items a mere 50 cents. Toilets are numerous, permanent fixtures, not portable johns with doors that shut with a clatter.

Scoreboards are prompt and up-to-date, manned by live people, not some electronic billboard in the woods making sounds like some animal with discomfort.

There is no pro-am, but the informal par-3 tournament on Wednesday gives spectators unable to make the annual badge list a chance to schmooze around with their heroes, both American and international.

Now, about us, the press. The facility, a permanent building, is the best at any sports event, thereby making up for the on-course restrictions. There is no herd of accompanists, mostly unnecessary, tramping down the fairway behind the players. While I'd love to be out there, as at any other tournament — sometimes I hate that I'm not — I approve of the practice. This is not any other tournament, and that is why it is great.

Heralded players win The Masters. Rarely ever does one of the ordinary foot soldiers of the tour slip into the green jacket on Sunday.

Therein lies another story, the respect, the awe in which The Masters is held by the players themselves.

"Not to be in The Masters is like being out of the world for a week," Doug Sanders once said before he grew into the Senior Tour.

One last thing, the holes have names. Not that other courses haven't christened their 18, but Tea Olive, Flowering Crab Apple, Yellow Jasmine, Carolina Cherry, White Dogwood and Golden Bell, all in strict correspondence with accompanying flora? Put all these wonderful characteristics together, and you have the finest sports event in the world, I say.

Bisher is not only one of the nation's top turf writers, he is also the co-owner, with ex-football star Sam Huff, of a two-year-old stabled in Maryland. "I hope he gets the idea that he's supposed to go fast," Bisher says.

April 4, 1993
Some serious horse racing
- - - - -

CUMMING, Ga. — Across the hillside came the wailing of the bag-pipes, something that sounds as if it needs oiling. Picnics were spread, tables were set by some, some with candlesticks and crystal things, and a thoroughbred spirit was in the air at John Wayt's Seven Branches Farm.

The 28th running of the Atlanta Steeplechase was called to order, with the finest of horses that like to run and leap over hedges.

Once upon a time this event was confused with al fresco partying.

One fellow I know said he doesn't go any more. "I don't like to drink in a pasture," he said.

What he doesn't understand, poor misguided fellow, is that this is sport. These are the finest horses in the world at what they do, "The finest quality field in every race of the last two years, I think," Ann Barker said, she the voice of steeplechase in The Racing Form.

Once again, as it turned out, what 15,000 patrons of the jump came to partake of was another celebration of Jonathan Sheppard. No man has dominated his sport as Jonathan Sheppard has dominated steeple-chasing the last 20 years, or since he fled the monotony of a brokerage house in London. Absolutely no man, or woman.

Jumpers he trained had won nine of the last 11 Atlanta Cup Handicaps, "about two miles over National Fences," as it is described in the program. This time he had brought three to make a run for it,

Double Bill, who surprised and won it last year; Runway Romance, with Blythe Miller up; and Ninepins, with Craig Thornton, the New Zealand import, aboard. Oddly enough, neither was suspected of being the horse most likely to win it.

The favorite was Warm Spell, a 5-year-old Northern Dancer grandson who won three of the four races he ran last year. Warm Spell is owned by John Griggs, a Kentucky veterinarian, and ridden by his son, Kirk, a lawyer by profession, a jockey for fun.

"That's racing as it should be," Sheppard said, "horse owned and trained by the father, ridden by the son."

He is a very fair man, this Sheppard, though I suppose it is easy to be fair when the world is your oyster. He was speaking again, after the race was over and Ninepins, odds of 3-1 to Warm Spell's 3-2, had won: "I was watching with my son, who doesn't get to the track very much. I had told him Warm Spell would win, he is so strong. They were on the backstretch and I said, 'Watch him, there he goes,' and Warm Spell made a big move, and just as I said it, he hit the hedge and went down. There is no doubt in my mind that he would have won the race."

Ninepins still had one more issue to settle. Jeff Teter, aboard

Victorian Hill, the steeplechase money champion of all time, protested that Ninepins had interfered on the turn for home. Janet Elliot, his trainer, was seething. This is the continuation of a long-term rivalry between Sheppard and Elliot, last trainer to beat Sheppard at his game.

"That Craig Thornton," she said, "he shoved my horse all over the track. He is such a rough rider."

Thornton was set down at Saratoga for rough riding last year, but the stewards didn't see it the Teter-Elliott way after reviewing the film. The verdict stood and the bulk of the $100,000 Robinson-Humphrey purse went to Sheppard and his client, Ed Sawyer, a patron of the arts in Albany, N.Y. Ninepin, now 6 years old, came to Sheppard last year after Swyer bought him at auction in Ireland and represents a one-horse stable after a previous unhappy experience in flat racing.

"He bought a horse for $100,000, but after a few races the trainer advised him to sell him, that he was not sound and wouldn't last very long," Sheppard said. "He sold the horse, just about broke even, and you know what the horse's name was? Black Tie Affair."

Black Tie Affair won the Breeders Cup Classic and became horse of the year in 1991.

Sheppard owns Atlanta, now that he has won 10 of the last 12 Cups, and heaven knows how many other races at Seven Branches, two more sandwiched around the main event Saturday, Dum Crambo in the third and Pre Op Scrub in the fifth. The protest lodged by Teter is a continuation of a peculiar series involving the two jumpers, Ninepins and Victorian Hill. In the Grand National at Far Hills, N.J., last year, an inquiry was called when Teter claimed that Circuit Bar, who finished first, had interfered with "Vic," who finished third.

This time the protest was upheld. Circuit Bar was dropped to third and the horse that finished second was placed first. His name was, and is, Ninepins.

The Braves were baseball's best. But what other writer could see the World Series victory from Bisher's special perspective? Who else wrote the definitive history of the team's legal wranglings to get out of Milwaukee and construct the first of two homes on Capitol Avenue, and is Hank Aaron's biographer? Who else could watch Greg Maddux, Tom Glavine and John Smoltz, and see in his mind's eye Warren Spahn, Johnny Sain, Tony Cloninger and Phil Niekro? Interview Bobby Cox and think of Fred Haney, Bobby Bragan and Luman Harris? Who else in the press box had been born when Babe Ruth was still a pitcher?

Oct. 29, 1995
World champion at last
- - - - -

The world stopped turning last night. The sun came up at midnight.

Atlanta turned the other cheek and didn't get slapped. The Braves went to bed — if they went to bed at all — champions of the baseball world, to go with the "Miracle Braves" of Boston and the Milwaukee Braves of Wisconsin. Of 1914, of 1957 and of 1995.

Now the deed has been done. Now it can be told, if in this pandemonium, this raging ecstasy, this delirium, it can be told at all.

In this city raised from the ashes of war now flies the most coveted flag in baseball. It has been 30 seasons coming, since the franchise left Milwaukee and took up housekeeping among us. For all those years of deprivation, for all those dismal seasons spent in the squalor of the second division — eight times they finished last — this was the payback.

To all those fans of the Southeast, who fell under the severe critique of David Justice, there was another payback. In an evening heavily laden with irony, the irony of it all was that the man who provided the necessary offense was Himself — David Justice, this fellow who looks to the stands for his inspiration. For 5 1/2 innings it had been a scoreless game, an enthralling standoff between Tom Glavine and Dennis Martinez, until Justice led off the Atlanta sixth with a tall home run over the right field fence. It would turn out to be the only run of the game.

Now for the other twist: The victim was the left-handed Jim Poole, who continued a losing day for Georgia Tech, his alma mater, football

BOBBY COX

victim of Clemson University at Bobby Dodd Stadium. Poole had done his job in the fifth, following Martinez to the mound and striking out Fred McGriff on three pitches. Then all that irony was condensed into the one moment he faced Justice, who had come up a rookie while Poole was getting his pitching education across town.

On the thin edge of that one-run margin, the Braves walked a tightrope through the last three innings, bearing out still another irony. In a Series role that had been reserved for Greg Maddux, Tom Glavine applied the masterful finishing touch with a brilliant one-hitter. The one hit was a soft fly that Tony Pena dropped in right-centerfield opening the sixth inning. He was forced at second, and the Indians had only one more base runner the rest of the night.

What made this finale the fitting event that it was, was the magnificence of it. It was baseball at its very finest, from the pitching to the defense, to which the hitless wonder, Rafael Belliard, applied the signature, running down Kenny Lofton's foul over the left field line at breakneck speed, first out of the ninth inning with Mark Wohlers closing it out. The last was Carlos Baerga's fly to Marquis Grissom in left-center field, upon which this old stadium exploded into one wild burst of emotion. Sanity, however, did prevail.

"30 Years of Waiting Ends Tonight," read a homemade banner spread behind home plate before the game, and, afterward, while the emotionally wrought fans stood singing in the stands. It wasn't a song I could make out, but that didn't matter. It was a song of joy and fruition.

And what a year it has been for the man behind it all. Ted Turner sat in the field box near the Braves dugout with a few of his friends, a most diverse group including a former president, Jimmy Carter, and Newt Gingrich, speaker of the House, and Turner's wife, Jane Fonda. The Braves win the pennant and TBS has grown into exciting manhood, all for a guy who started on a shoestring, and who bought the Braves in 1976, not knowing a passed ball from a foul ball. To him, the risk-taker, goes Atlanta's standing ovation.

It hasn't been a ride across a totally barren field. The Braves won the National League West in 1969, again in 1982, before turning the '90s into their decade. A World Series in '91 and a World Series in '92, a division championship in 1993, followed by the Year of the Strikers.

Bobby Cox had had a near-miss when he managed Toronto in the American League. Was this his doom? A career of near-misses.

Now his destiny has been met. This was the manager Ted Turner fired in 1981, returned as general manager, then back to the field in 1990, then moved from worst to first in 1991. What a lovely diary.

"I'd hire him again," Turner said the day he announced his firing. He was as good as his word.

They're down on the field now, celebrating. Steve Avery with his shirt-tail out, Chipper Jones running along the tarpaulin roll, David Justice telling television how much he really loves Atlanta fans, and the world can start turning again.

The impetus for the Atlanta Olympics can be traced to the city's rich history in Sports, and also to the genius of Bisher. While his counterparts in other Southern cities remained regionally important, he became a globe-trotter. Every column he wrote transcending our little corner of the world over five decades sent Atlantans a message, relayed from his fellow editors Henry Grady and Ralph McGill. It is this: instead of provincialism and isolationism, think globally. When the Olympics finally arrived, a small army of newsmen and women, drawn locally and from Cox Newspapers, was on hand to cover it. This column was Bisher's own full blessing of the event.

July 21, 1996
Let the Games begin

- - - - -

It's a miracle! The cow jumped over the moon. The tortoise beat the hare again.

Somebody kissed a frog and it turned into a beautiful princess. Moving with the speed of light, leaping tall buildings, repelling flying bullets, it was SuperPayne, standing in the midst of it all, surrounded by a sea of color representing 197 nations and a stadium rocking with enthusiasm.

William Porter Payne Jr. — Billy to you and me, and Martha — said to Juan Antonio Samaranch, the elfin Spaniard who runs the International Olympic Committee, "We extend to you a very warm welcome." And he delivered, up to 90 degrees. (His daddy, Porter Payne, a burly all-star lineman at Georgia who died too young, would have been more than proud.)

There it was, the Opening Ceremony spread out for all the world to see on what, just over two years ago, was a swatch of land only freshly disturbed by construction. Now what had risen from the earth was a skeletal queen, her ribs and limbs mostly obscured by 84,000 or so who had endured the strenuousness of getting there, and then finally departing 40 minutes behind schedule.

The 12:01 torch lighting had actually taken place about 12:26 with the major surprise of the ceremony. The mystery of how the caldron would be ignited was finally revealed, after one false lead after another, like an Agatha Christie theme. First, came Al Oerter delivering the flame to the stadium, then Evander Holyfield sharing a stadium run with Paraskevi Patoulidou, the female hurdler who had won Greece's first gold medal in years at Barcelona — an olive branch to Athens, the disappointed bidder — then to Janet Evans, the swimmer who negotiated the ramp to place the torch in the quivering hands of Muhammad Ali, Cassius Clay when he won the light heavyweight gold in 1960, once the self-proclaimed "Greatest" now under the withering effects of Parkinson's disease.

He moved carefully with the torch, then applied it to the wire that lifted it to the caldron, and the flame flared, to burn for two weeks, another triumph in the service of Atlanta Gas Light.

Also, not to be overlooked, those creative engineers at Georgia Tech who worked a year to perfect a torch that would survive the staggering journey from Greece to Capitol Avenue, weeks by air, water, wheel and foot. Malcolm Grear designed it; Dr. Sam Shelton and staff of five turned it into an instrument to hold fuel for 45 minutes, withstand taxing elements, large enough to be visible at a distance but small enough to be safe for the carriers, weight about three pounds.

For all the dancing and wind-blown effects, the parade is the thing. It began, as is tradition, with the Greek delegation, the host team bringing up the rear, from Afghanistan to Zimbabwe in between; with 70 nations that have never won a medal; several new members created by nations reshaping themselves, including the "other" Georgia, now under new management; military enemies but Olympic friends marching in happiness next to one another; and ranging in size from Cook Islands, with three, to the U.S. with 600-and-something.

A lingering question: I wonder what time the last spectator got home. Otherwise, is Atlanta ready? So far, so good. Let the Games go on.

Furman Bisher talking to Ernie Harwell, longtime Detroit Tigers
announcer (left) and Bill White, National League president

Bisher and his fellow columnist, Lewis Grizzard

Bisher, Atlanta mayor Ivan Allen Jr. and Atlanta Braves
chairman William C. Bartholomay

In the newspaper's weekly "I Beat Bisher" competition, readers tried to predict the outcome of college football games as well as the sports editor had done. Beat Bisher and you received a t-shirt, tie him and you got a bumper sticker. In this photo, Bisher is in Moscow and has just affixed one of the bumper stickers to a Russian taxicab. A Coca-Cola official took the picture.

Bisher while heading up the Easter Seal Christmas drive

Celestine Sibley and Eleanor Roosevelt. "We shared the platform in a panel discussion at old Wesley Memorial Church," she says.

Sibley with Groucho Marx during one of her junkets to Hollywood in the early 1950s to interview the stars. "He was making a comedy called 'Three on a Horse' and was fun to talk to," she recalls.

91

Sibley at home at Sweet Apple cabin

Sibley's beat for a half-century, the world of Atlanta emanating
from Forsyth and Peachtree

Celestine Sibley, 1959

CELESTINE SIBLEY

The Atlanta Constitution 1941-82
The Atlanta Journal-Constitutution 1982 to present

Demands for raw materials led the nations fighting World War II to ration consumer goods. The conflict had ended 16 days earlier, but rationing remained in force as The Constitution*'s new columnist appealed to the local board for help with a family emergency. Did Jimmy ever get new shoes? "He must have," Sibley recalls, "he had to go to school."*

Sept. 18, 1945
Letter to the Ration Board

- - - - -

Members of the Fulton County Ration Board (Shoe Division)

Dear Sirs:

To begin with, we might as well admit the whole thing was ridiculous and inexcusable and there probably isn't a thing an august body such as yours can do about it, saying you wanted to. All those governmental rules and regulations and stuff — and besides, you do have a solemn patriotic duty to see that such shoes as there are get evenly distributed.

But, gentlemen, Jimmy needs a new pair of shoes! He needs 'em bad. His feet are on the ground, absolutely and irrevocably. He's actually a barefoot boy and he got that way — stop me if you've heard this before — by loving a dog not wisely but too well.

Now I know nearly everybody has a perfectly logical excuse for applying for an extra shoe ticket. (Down in Pensacola a ration board member told us if everybody who said they had dropped their shoes overboard while fishing or boating or riding the ferry was telling the truth, there's enough leather in Pensacola Bay to provide a new hide for every cow in Texas.) Anyhow, I make no claim that this application for a shoe stamp is logical. But it's true, if absurd.

You see, out in Buckhead on Martina Drive there's a dog, a foolish looking highly unpedigreed pup named Jim. Jim would never make Ruth Stanton Cogill's dog column and probably not the lost-stolen-strayed-liberal reward department, either. He's just a plain dog, a little

black, a little brindle, a touch of white on one or two of his big feet and two copper spots around his eyes that give him an oddly quizzical expression — sort of like a man peering at the world through a pair of misplaced monocles and finding what he sees extremely amusing. Well, that's Jim, gentlemen, and if you are not interested I don't blame you.

The point is that Jimmy, the boy, was interested in Jim — too interested. You see Jimmy, like the dog, Jim, is not particularly distinguished. Just a freckle-faced boy with a cowlick and long legs and hands and feet that are bigger than you'd think they'd be. But Jimmy has lived six years of his life without a dog and when he met Jim it suddenly got to be more than he could stand. He loved Jim and Jim, unquestionably animal that he is, loved back. For hours they sat in the back yard in silent communion, Jimmy rubbing Jim's droopy hound's ears and Jim with a companionable paw on Jimmy's scuffed-up knee.

The weather was hot and Jim's big feet, all four of them, were bare and maybe you gentlemen can understand how, after a while, Jimmy's new shoes, his one and only pair, got to fretting his feet. Anyhow he took 'em off and that was last week and school has started and all the other boys in high first have new school shoes and Jimmy, like Deedle-Deedle-Dumpling-My-Son-John is walking around with one shoe off and one shoe on.

Now you gentlemen understand Jimmy doesn't care. He likes to go around barefoot. And besides he thinks what Jim did was simply captivating. You could see him swelling with pride as he reported it.

"You know what Jim did?" he said. "He took one of my shoes in his mouth and trotted off with it. Just like it was a bone!"

"And probably buried it like it was a bone, too," commented one of the neighbors.

Anyhow we've held treasure hunts up and down Martina Drive, gentlemen of the ration board (shoe division), digging up slews of old prewar steak bones and other odd shoes of 1928 vintage, but no brown oxfords, left foot, size 2-B. We held solemn conclave around Jim, all the while noting that the leaves of the muscadine vine are turning yellow and there's an unmistakable promise of an early — and probably frosty fall in the air. But it's all to no avail.

Jim just smiles around his copper colored monocles and looks coy. Is there anything you gentlemen can do, either about another ration stamp or a coy dog?

Any help in this problem which is, admittedly, above and beyond your call of duty, will be sincerely appreciated by:

Yours very truly,

JIMMY'S MOTHER

"The first trips I ever took by plane from Atlanta were from that little yellow stucco terminal," Sibley recalls. She wrote this firsthand account of the unveiling of the new postwar facility by Mayor William B. Hartsfield. Its simple building materials belie the grandeur of the giant midfield terminal now on the site and named for the former mayor.

July 27, 1947 news story
Air terminal looms as 'the finest'

- - - - -

"The best darned temporary passenger terminal in the nation" soon will be open to the air-traveling public out at the Municipal Airport.

That's what city officials are saying about the $200,000 structure which is 85 percent completed on the Army ramp at the west end of the city's airport. Counter space already has been alloted two airlines and the city is considering contracting for the operation of the restaurant which, according to Mayor Hartsfield, is to offer not routine terminal fare but "make-'em-want-to-come-back southern cookery."

The terminal, airport officials said, will be clearly marked "Atlanta-Temporary Passenger Terminal" to stave off any suggestions for further streamlining but frankly, they are expecting no complaints. The make-do way station of the airways may have to last for years, at least until the federal government can be prevailed upon to match the $3,000,000 raised by bond issue to build a new atom-age terminal.

Hangaresque in architecture, the terminal can be converted into a hangar by the simple trick of knocking out one end and substituting sliding doors and removing a few interior partitions. It is of concrete brick structure with a metal roof and has within its 125-by-200-foot exterior the most spacious lobby and lounges city officials have found anywhere in the nation.

The temporary terminal will take over the airline passenger activities now being handled at the Administration Building which was erected in 1931, long before Atlanta became one of the nation's busiest airports. The office, weather bureau and control tower will continue to operate in the present building, along with the restaurant which is patronized largely by airport workers.

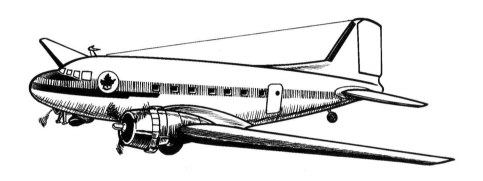

The ramps, which the city inherited from the Army at the close of the war, were the primary reason for locating the temporary terminal at the west end of the field. When it has outlived its usefulness as a passenger terminal the big hangar may well serve as a cargo terminal, airport authorities point out.

So far the space inside the big hangar has had only a slight dent made in it by the demands of the two airlines, Delta and Eastern, who will have ticket counters, offices and baggage-handling facilities.

An area at the east end, measuring 49 by 59 feet, will serve as a lounge with linoleum tile covering its floor and comfortable divans and desks deployed at graceful intervals to rest the weary travelers. There will be 16 telephones, several telegraph wires, rest rooms and a barber shop.

Initial plans for the terminal, back in the days when the $6,000,000 new administration building seemed an early prospect, called for leaving the rafters and metal ceiling exposed. Since then scrap wallboard, salvaged from Army installations, has been brought in and used as ceiling and partitions. Over the ticket offices of the airlines Mayor Hartsfield visualizes a photographic mural to pique visitors' interest in Atlanta. He is discussing the layout with several local artists and photographers and the central theme is expected to be Atlanta's skyline with side shots of such points of interest as Stone Mountain and the Cyclorama.

A wooden structure formerly used as an Army recreation hall will be moved over beside the terminal to house the airport post office, which at present employs 60 people sorting and re-routing air-mail.

Bulldozers have just been brought in to level off driveways and dig parking space out of the hillside on the city side of the hangar.

Georgians liked to refer to Atlanta's hospital affectionately as "The Grady," and one patron had this novel idea for taking care of his wife's bill. However, "I don't believe it's like that anymore," Celestine Sibley says.

Aug. 24, 1947 news story
Hospital regrets losing goat deal

- - - - -

Grady Hospital's administrative forces had to admit Saturday they weren't on their toes.

Several weeks ago they were offered a milk goat in exchange for saving a woman's life, but their acceptance was so slow coming the goat donor, W. B. Miller, reported Saturday he had withdrawn his offer.

"Too bad," hospital administrators said sadly. "We just couldn't make up our minds whether to turn the goat over to the business office or over to the dietary department."

Goat owner Miller took the appearance of a reporter and a photographer at his asphalt-can residence near Adamsville as a belated show of interest on the hospital's part and he was genuinely regretful.

"Now I'm just as sorry as I can be I didn't hold that goat for the Grady," Miller declared. "I sold her for $10 and she was worth three times the price. As good a milker as you ever saw — five quarts a day if she was fed right."

Old Belle, the milk goat, was the first payment Mr. Miller had to make on what he felt was a long-standing account at Grady Hospital.

"The Grady saved my wife's life," he said, "and there's hardly a one of my people who haven't been there for one thing or another. I was there myself once — my wife was there three times — and nearly all my brothers and my sisters and their children have been treated there. Yes, sir, offering them Old Belle was little enough to do. And if they're still

W.B. MILLER AND HIS GOAT

interested, well, I'm going to see if I can't get my hands on another good milker for them."

Miller and his wife, Lula, live on a rutted red slope off Fairburn Road in a three-room house built entirely out of asphalt cans cut, straightened out and nailed to a framework of timbers from trees felled on the site.

"Paid five cents apiece for the asphalt cans," Mr. Miller explained, "and me and my brother did all the work ourselves. Only leaks in two places."

Although the little structure, now seven years old, has dirt floors, it is wired for electricity and by pulling a string the householder turns on a light, a radio and an electric fan. The clean swept yard is bright with beds of flowers and a well down the hill and an asphalt can outhouse provide plumbing facilities.

A well-fed cow and a mule occupy stalls in the garden and a cat and a dog share space under the stove. There are animals a-plenty but Mr. Miller is still sad over the untimely sale of "Belle."

"Slick as a butter mold, she was," he sighed. "Woulda been a fine hospital goat."

Sibley's coverage of this sensational trial gripped The Constitution's readers. "People still mention that case to me, still remember John Wallace as a man who really ran his county, a sinister man," says Sibley. After the trial, in his cell at Atlanta's Fulton Tower prison, Wallace confidently predicted to Sibley that his death sentence would never be carried out. He was wrong.

June 19, 1948 news story
Wallace given death chair sentence

- - - - -

NEWNAN, Ga., June 18 — John Wallace, prominent Meriwether County farmer, today was found guilty of murder in the "burned bones" slaying of William H. (alias Wilson) Turner and sentenced to die in the electric chair July 30.

A Coweta County jury arrived at a verdict of guilty at 5:10 p.m., after deliberating an hour and 10 minutes and listening to testimony and arguments five days. Judge Samuel J. Boykin, of Carrollton, passed sentence immediately.

Coatless, wearing rumpled gabardine trousers and a shirt, Wallace stood before the bench between his attorneys to hear the death sentence. Judge Boykin asked if he had anything to say and Wallace turned to Gus Huddleston, a member of his counsel from Greenville, and whispered: "Should I say anything?"

Huddleston shook his head and Judge Boykin passed sentence. Later Huddleston reiterated his intention of filing a motion for a new trial. Other defendants indicted jointly with Wallace for the April 20 slaying of Turner will go to trial at 10 a.m. Monday. They include Herring Sivell, Tom Strickland, Wallace's cousin; Henry Mobley, and two Negroes who testified against Wallace, Robert Lee Cates and Albert Brooks.

Although the courtroom was crowded, a dead silence greeted the reading of the verdict. Judge Boykin had previously warned against demonstrations of any kind but even after he left the bench the crowds surged sluggishly and without any apparent emotion around the rail. Wallace sat quietly for a moment, talking with his attorneys and chewing gum.

Asked if he had any statement to make, he said, "not just now. This is a serious time. Maybe later."

As he was leaving the courtroom, a little gray-haired woman tugged at his coat sleeve and said, "If there's anything we can do, John..." He smiled at her and said, "Thank you, I'll let you know."

Since Wallace in his talking marathon of more than six hours of Thursday completely exonerated the other defendants in the case, Coweta County citizens are speculating as to whether the three white men will go to trial on murder charges or be allowed to enter pleas of guilty to lesser offenses. Wallace admitted shooting Turner "accidentally" at an old abandoned well the afternoon of April 20, after a more than five-hour build-up in which he emphasized his fear that Turner would "get me in trouble with his whiskey-making" and charged the young man with "stealing my cows and threatening my security."

Wallace emphatically denied that Turner died from blows received about the head at a Coweta tourist camp and he did not touch upon the grisly details of the recovery of Turner's body from the well and cremation on a pyre in the swamp.

"My mind went blank," Wallace said.

Courthouse attachees confidently expected Wallace's attorneys to seek a change of venue on the ground that Turner was slain in Meriwether County and Judge Boykin instructed the jury to decide that issue first. Venue, he said, was a "material allegation" in the indictment and unless that was proven it was the jury's duty to acquit. The court's charge left only three verdicts open to the jury: guilty, guilty with a recommendation for mercy, or not guilty.

Huddleston, who with A.L. Henson, of Atlanta, served as leading counsel for Wallace, described the case as "attracting more attention in this state than any trial since the Leo Frank case." Henson accused the state of making the trial a "Hollywood scenario come to life" and attacked both expert testimony and the testimony of eyewitnesses who, he said, had prejudice "popping out of them like fleas on a dog."

Sol. Gen. Luther M. Wyatt bolstered the state's contention that Turner was actually killed in Coweta County with the testimony of rebuttal witnesses who said there was no evidence of blood or brain tissue on the ground around the old well and the position of the body in the well indicated it had been dead for some time before it was placed in there. Special prosecutor Meyer Goldberg asked the death penalty. Turning to Wallace, he thundered, "If you want to keep your trial in your county, Wallace, you keep your devilment, you keep your murder in your county."

On the tumultuous day that a session of the Georgia General Assembly ended, the solons "threw papers in the air, and drank a lot of whiskey," Sibley recalls. She was The Constitution'*s legislative reporter from 1958 to 1978, during five administrations. Often she took "gallop polls," she liked to say, by "galloping all over the capitol."*

Feb. 2, 1949 news story
Horseplay abounds as legislature curtain drops

- - - - -

Handshakes, horseplay and hilarity, unlimited, filled the House yesterday as weary legislators, some of them bitterly disillusioned, waited out the final working hours of the Senate before the historic moment when the doors of both houses were flung open and they adjourned simultaneously at 6:13 p.m.

Business was finished in the House about 3 p.m. Many representatives went home immediately afterwards but those who remained with mock gravity introduced comic bills and resolutions, sang barber shop harmony and wildly cheered their more gifted colleagues in imitations.

The floor was littered with paper. A few munched peanuts and candy. Some of the older, more dignified members took their wives and children around the floor introducing them to friends. But for the most part remaining members lounged in their chairs and asked only to be amused.

Rep. Clifford Cranford, of Coweta, the best baritone in the House, grasped the microphone and led the harmony with such songs as "Huggin' and Chalkin'," "I Want a Girl Just Like the Girl that Married Dear Old Dad" and "When Irish Eyes Are Smilin'." He was joined in the close harmony section by Frank Gross and Muggsy Smith.

Rep. Elliott Hagan, of Screven, responding reluctantly to the insistent applause of his colleagues, brought an unexpectedly serious moment to the House by reviving his imitation of President Roosevelt's fireside chats. Then brushing his hair down on his forehead, he said soberly:

EUGENE TALMADGE

"I don't believe 'Ole Gene' himself would mind this."

Members of the House rallied quickly and egged him on with the old Talmadge rally cry, "Tell 'em about it, Gene!" Hagan snorted and wheeled and snapped his suspenders in pantomime and revived such Talmadge oldies as this: "The poor man in Georgia ain't got but three friends left — God Almighty, Sears-Roebuck and Eugene Talmadge!"

He was followed by blind Rep. Vaughn Terrell, of Rome, who imitated such radio personages as Bob Burns, and by Miss Elsie Peacock, secretary of Speaker Fred Hand, who gave a lively, highly personalized imitation of Minnie Pearl.

During the lull in the variety show, Rep. Alex Boone, of Wilkinson County, introduced a resolution to keep the House in session till a bill was passed providing wigs and a $10,000 maintenance fee for all the bald-headed men in Georgia. The resolution, which wig-wearing Rep. Boone said was suggested to him by Jack Tarver, associate editor of *The Constitution*, was suitably referred to a Wig Committee.

At 6 p.m. adjournment resolutions were exchanged and at 6:10 p.m. the doors of both houses were swung open and Speaker Hand faced Marvin Griffin, president of the Senate, across the length of the capitol. Both men raised their handkerchiefs and dropped them slowly and then Speaker Hand banged his gavel and cried:

"The House of Representatives stands adjourned to 10 o'clock the morning of Jan. 16, 1950."

The setting for what is perhaps Sibley's best-known work was North Avenue's Majestic Diner, long since torn down. The main player in the drama was her daughter, Mary. This column won the Christopher Award, including a $2,000 cash prize. Here is Sibley at her best.

April 8, 1951
A little girl asks the blessing

- - - - -

The lunch counter had that stainless steel and nickle shine indigenous to lunch counters — and in the soft early morning light it looked clean and impersonal but sort of cheerful. We sat there listening to the hiss of the waffle iron, watching the steamy breath of the coffee urn spiraling upward and wondering if Dr. Thornwell Jacobs had thought to include such a place in his Civilization Crypt.

No future civilization can get any idea of what life in the 20th Century was like unless he could see 20-odd citizens lined up on stools at a gleaming eatery early in the morning. We looked at these, shoulders hunched over the "two-fresh-eggs-and-buttered toast" special faces reflected here and there in coffee urns and stainless steel panels.

There were college students, fugitives from fraternity house cuisine, a somber-looking man with a briefcase (could it be his wife was a late-sleeper?), two young nurses, a little rumpled and hollow-eyed after a night on duty at the nearby hospital, a family with a little girl and a sullen teenager impartially distributing lipstick between her coffee cup and cigarette.

The lunchroom was quiet except for the occasional sharp crack of an eggshell in the counterman's expert hand, the sputter of frying bacon and the bored voice of a customer, ordering more coffee. The counterman turned a radio on a shelf up a little and war news clattered out. New raids on Communist air bases in Manchuria, possibility of Reds massing to send "full air power into Korea." Abruptly he switched it off and stood absently wiping the already spotless counter.

We thought of his customers, 20-odd people, each engrossed in his own thoughts, encased in his own shell — inconspicuous, anonymous, brought together by nothing more binding than the tribal custom of eating in the morning. They did not even have real, ravening hunger in common... just eating because people do.

And then at the end of the counter the little girl said in a carrying voice, "Mother, don't we ask the blessing here?"

The counterman stopped wiping and grinned at her suddenly.

"Sure we do, sister," he said. "You say it."

She bowed her smooth little head. The young counterman turned and glared briefly at his customers and bowed his head, too. Up and down the counter heads went down, the nurses, the students, the man with the briefcase and then, slowly, the teenager.

The breathless little voice was loud in the room:

"God is great, God is good. Let us thank Him for our food. By His hand we are fed, He gives to us our daily bread. Amen."

Heads went up along the counter. Eating was resumed but somehow the atmosphere had subtly changed. The man with the briefcase smiled and remarked to the nurses that he had a new baby in their hospital. Conversation became general. The counterman smiled at the students and said, "Well, I won't be seeing you after this week. I reckon I'm going to Korea." They paused, paying their check, to talk with him about it. Somehow a tenuous bond of friendliness and mutual confidence had grown up in the room and the little girl, oblivious to what she had done, lathered her waffle with syrup and ate it happily.

"It was many minutes before the crack of lightning and the roar of wind and rain let the whole story come through. Dr. Martin Luther King Jr., a kind man, an eloquent man, gone." This column ran five days after King's assassination, and in it Sibley revealed a personal encounter with the civil rights leader.

April 9, 1968
In the rain by a Mississippi truck stop
- - - - -

It's odd how the human mind can get used to a monstrous tragedy. First there's shock and disbelief and then grief and then I guess for everybody there comes a time of trying to cope with a hideous memory by fitting it into the homely setting of one's personal life. You know how people remember exactly where they were and what they were doing when they received terrible news. "The baby was sick and I was filling the croup kettle when I heard about Pearl Harbor on the radio"... "I was mopping the floor when a neighbor called across the street and told me President Roosevelt was dead"... "I stopped by the florist to buy some flowers and she said, 'Did you know about somebody shooting John Kennedy?'"

It is the same with the death of Martin Luther King Jr. The fact of his assassination is no less terrible but to accept it people somehow have to go back and tell you how it was with them when they heard the news.

I was driving along a Mississippi road in the dark with rain beating against the windshield and the lightning flashing wildly across the sky. Static made me turn off the radio but it was lonesome on the dark rain-swept highway. (John, the 5-year-old grandchild, had been asleep on the back seat since we stopped for a hamburger in Montgomery.) So I fiddled with the dial hoping for news and then I got a fragment or two about a shooting somewhere. It was many minutes before the crack of the lightning and the roar of wind and rain let the whole story come through. Dr. Martin Luther King Jr., a kind man, an eloquent man, gone.

The lights of a truck stop were just ahead and I pulled off and sat there. The impulse of all newspaper reporters is to call the office when news of a great moment happens — to ask "Do you need me? Shall I

DR. MARTIN LUTHER KING JR.

come in?" But I was more than 300 miles away with a sleeping child on the back seat and other children ahead, waiting for me. The need for any services of mine would be over by the time I could get back so I sat there by the Mississippi truck stop watching the rain make mud of the parking area, watching the big trucks pull in to wait out the rain, and thinking about Dr. King.

My personal acquaintance with him was so slight. He had done me a favor once and I couldn't remember if I'd ever thanked him for it. My youngest daughter was but 14 or 15 at the time and urgently concerned to have a hand in making things better for downtrodden people. It wasn't enough to carry a sign with pickets. She wanted to fill our house with hungry and homeless people. She wanted to be a freedom rider. And one day when I thought she was safe in summer school, making up history which she was failing, she caught a bus for Montgomery.

Frightened and frantic I called Dr. King. With his own people being beaten and killed my concern for my little white child might well have amused him. It didn't. "She's got to LEARN history before she can MAKE it!" I wailed. He agreed. He said he would find her and talk to her and within a few hours one of his aides took her to the Montgomery airport, boarded a plane with her and brought her home.

Sitting there by the truck stop I wished I had done something to help his cause. And I wasn't even sure I'd said thank you.

Sibley and Constitution *editor Ralph McGill covered the court proceedings in Memphis for James Earl Ray, convicted killer of Martin Luther King Jr. Decades later, Sibley lived to see the case re-opened by a federal court. But the eyewitness to Ray's 1969 plea says today, "He's guilty, as guilty as he can be."*

March 11, 1969 news story
James Earl Ray sentenced to 99 years

- - - - -

MEMPHIS, Tenn. — James Earl Ray, who has seen a lot of prisons and escaped the last with a vow never to return, Monday chose the longest jail sentence of all — 99 years — rather than stand trial for the slaying of Atlanta civil rights leader Dr. Martin Luther King Jr.

Defense attorney Percy Foreman told a hastily empaneled jury that Ray's choice represented "the extreme penalty short of one — death," and he expressed the opinion that there is "no punishment at all in death except for the moment it comes."

Under Tennessee law Ray will have to serve 33 of the 99 years before he will be eligible for a parole. If the sentence had been life imprisonment, he could have applied for a parole in 13 years.

Sheriff William Morris said Ray will be transferred to the state penitentiary in Nashville "anytime now, as soon as the governor says he is ready for him." The penitentiary is understood to be installing super security precautions similar to the ones under which Ray has been incarcerated in Shelby County Jail.

Shelby Criminal Court Judge W. Preston Battle passed sentence on Ray at 12:10 p.m. at the end of what had promised to be one of the most sensational murder trials of the decade and turned out to be one of the most anticlimactic. The verdict and the sentence were agreed upon

117

before court opened but Tennessee laws require that the jury hear enough evidence to confirm both.

The jury of men, two of them Negroes, agreed to accept both the plea of guilty and the 99-year sentence before they were sworn in. Then they heard the testimony of four witnesses — two of them friends of Dr. King and eyewitnesses to his slaying last April 4; the county medical examiner, a city detective and an FBI agent.

JAMES EARL RAY

The rest of the details of Ray's cross-continent wanderings before and after the shooting of King, his abandonment of a white Mustang automobile in Atlanta, his flight from Canada and subsequent arrest in London were summarized to the jury in a narrative of stipulations agreed to by attorneys from both sides.

Ray spoke only half a dozen times during the trial. "Yes sir... yes sir... yes sir!" he said over and over in answer to Judge Battle's questions as to whether he entered his guilty plea "with free will and full understanding of its meaning and consequences."

Once when Judge Battle asked if he had acted out of pressure or desire to protect someone else, Ray replied shortly, "I'm pleading guilty!"

Later, when his attorney told the jury that he, Foreman, was convinced that Ray acted alone and not in a conspiracy to kill King, Ray stood up and mumbled that he wanted to "add" something about "not agreeing with" Atty. Gen. Ramsey Clark and FBI Chief J. Edgar Hoover.

Foreman and Judge Battle looked puzzled and both again asked him if he still wanted to plead guilty.

"Yes sir, yes sir," said Ray, sitting down.

Sibley had a special admiration for Georgia Sen. Richard B. Russell. She recalls: "One time we (The Constitution*) were kind of pumping him for president, and we had a parade at Five Points. I was in the press car. Someone said, 'He's colorless, what he needs is a wife and children.' I said, 'I'll volunteer. I'll let him marry me and my children.'"*

March 24, 1969
'Each small-seeming request'
- - - - -

The illness of Sen. Richard Russell has, I feel sure, set all his friends and neighbors in Georgia and probably people in all parts of the world thinking about him with special warmth and concern. The day the word that he had cancer reached the Georgia capitol you could hear people all over the place beginning sentences with "I remember..." They remember all kinds of things about him, important and trivial, funny and solemn. So many of them were inspired to run for public office by his example back in the 1930s when he stumped the state as a bright young reform candidate for governor.

He was my first Georgia politician. I had worked for the paper only a little while when I was sent to Winder to cover a speech by Sen. Russell at a barbecue. I don't remember the speech now but I remember the feeling I had about the tall, slender man who moved easily and comfortably among his old neighbors and friends. The smell of the smoke from the barbecue pit was rich and pungent with the blend of oak and hickory and succulent roast pork. Hound dogs flapped their tails from beneath parked cars and shade trees. Little children cried out and were hushed by an absent pat of the hand from a listening mother or a father. At the time I was impressed by the fact that Sen. Russell arrived without a retinue of aides and flunkies and that he was approachable.

There were times later when I was to approach him for favors for friends and the marvel to me was that he received each small-seeming request as if it were of the greatest importance and dealt with it with speed and efficiency.

SEN. RICHARD B. RUSSELL

There was the time the teenage daughter of a friend of mine was missing in Europe. She had been in school in Florence and had told her parents that she had just enough money to get to Paris for a holiday. They told her they would send money to her in care of American Express in Paris and to let them know that she had arrived there safely and collected it.

Days passed and they didn't hear from their daughter. They telephoned American Express in Paris to find that the money still waited for her there, uncollected. They didn't know a soul in Paris to whom they could appeal for help and finally the mother called me, assuming that newspaper friends would have connections in almost every corner of the world.

Oddly enough my newspaper friends who might have had Paris connections didn't take the problem seriously. They had the "Oh, she's having a good time, she'll turn up," approach.

Incensed because she was a child dear to me, too, I stalked to the telephone and called Sen. Russell at his home in Winder. He might have sighed a little to himself but he didn't laugh. He said, "Celestine, there are probably three million Americans in Paris this summer but we wouldn't want one little Georgia girl to be lost. I'll see what I can do."

Within 12 hours Sen. Russell's "connections" in Paris had found my young friend and had her telephone her frantic parents.

It was a small thing to take to so powerful and important a man, I realize now. But Sen. Russell didn't belittle it. He dealt with it. The picture of a great man is built of such little bits and pieces. No wonder so many of us grieve that he is ill and pray for his recovery.

William Holmes Borders, pastor of Atlanta's Wheat Street Baptist Church, annually portrayed Jesus Christ in the pageant "Behold the Man." In the late 1960s, it was staged with a cast of thousands at Atlanta-Fulton County Stadium. Celestine Sibley caught up with Rev. Borders during rehearsal. "No man is good enough for the role," Dr. Borders said.

April 22, 1969
'Too old, too black, too busy'

- - - - -

Theatrical warehouses are not common in this vicinity and the one down on Lee Street, where they are building sets and props for next Saturday's presentation of "Behold the Man" is full of wild and wonderful things — Roman soldiers' gear, headless papier-mache cherubim and chariots. It is also noisy with a lot of hammering and sawing and we had to sit in an oddly plush-covered trailer office to talk to Dr. William Holmes Borders, the man who will portray Christ in the pageant. (Plush-covered the trailer was, in an effort at sound-proofing.)

But it was all right because talking to the 62-year-old Negro Baptist preacher and civic leader is an experience which is even better than kibitzing on most theatrical productions. Dr. Borders, as everybody who knows him will tell you, is one of Atlanta's authentic sights and wonders.

He is the man they said was too old, too black and too busy to play the role of Jesus — and yet his performance last year was astoundingly moving to the thousands of people who packed the stadium and he has been asked to repeat it this year.

Old and black, the white-haired Negro preacher cheerfully admits to being. But too busy? Not for one moment!

"No man is good enough for the role," he says slowly in his deep rich baritone. "All you can do is to try."

And that Dr. Borders is doing and has been doing for months. The "lines" of the pageant, the words from the Bible, have been familiar to him most of his life. His father was a Baptist preacher — Swift Creek Baptist Church in Bibb County — and he has been one for 37 years. But he studies the role as assiduously as any young neophyte. When I arrived to interview him he had just been having a diction lesson from the director-author, Frank Roughton.

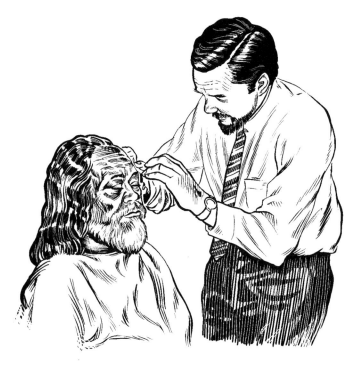

**REV. WILLIAM HOLMES BORDERS
IN PREPARATION FOR HIS ROLE AS JESUS CHRIST**

"Trying to learn to pronounce my 't's," he said, lifting a humorous eyebrow. "Now th-th-therefore…"

Perfect, unregional speech doesn't come easily to a man from Middle Georgia even if he is a graduate of Northwestern University and he wouldn't mind, except that he thinks the words of Jesus should be spoken in accents of "universality." But not, he hastens to add, at the sacrifice of "quality of thought, rhythm and balance."

Most actors who have played the role of Christ claim that it is a mystical experience that is deeply and personally affecting. Dr. Borders, who has preached the words of Jesus from the pulpit of Wheat Street Baptist Church every Sunday for 32 years, finds that trying to say them as Jesus might have said them is a special and different thing. He finds himself awakening at 3 and 4 o'clock in the morning and going over and over such words as "Thy faith has made thee whole" and finding them fresher and more meaningful than ever.

The opportunity to see this mighty pageant, sponsored by the Christian Council of Metropolitan Atlanta and employing the talents of 600 other actors and 3,000 singers, white and black, will be available again Saturday and Sunday nights, starting at 8 p.m. Tickets range in price from $1.50 to $5.50 and may be bought at a lot of grocery stores and other places. Call the Christian Council if you need the name of one.

No other columns by Celestine Sibley are as beloved as those written about Christmas and her family. In this memorable installment,
all of Sibley's preconceived notions about the type of tree to get,
when to decorate it, and the need for simple ornamentation are
sacrificed in the name of making her grandchildren happy.

Dec. 16, 1969
The living tree

- - - - -

Well, I've finally thrown in the towel on Christmas trees. It took two
generations to beat me down but beat I am. All my lifelong notions
about The Right Christmas Tree have gone a-glimmering. Two small
children, caught up in a tangle of uncertainties about Christmas, did it.

To begin with, since my own childhood I've held that the only kind
of Christmas tree to have was pine or maybe cedar. Balsams and hem-
locks and other store-bought trees were for other people, not for those
of us who lived within reach of native Southern pine and cedar.

The time you put up a Christmas tree was of major importance to me.
The Christmas trees of my childhood miraculously appeared on
Christmas morning and not a minute sooner. When I was older and able
to participate in getting and decorating a tree it became a ritual of
Christmas Eve, the going to the woods with a bearded old Cajun fellow
called "Pet" in his ox cart and hauling the tree home and setting it up
and then the whole family pitching in to "dress" it.

That way the "new" of the Christmas tree lasted for days and days. But
by the time I had children of my own the trend was toward more of
Christmas faster — so we started getting our trees earlier. I finally settled
for the Sunday before Christmas and managed to hold out on that until
this very year. Since I moved to Sweet Apple I've developed a whole set

of prejudices about ornaments. Real candles in little tin holders, instead of the electric kind, and homemade pretties instead of plastic and glitter.

But now... well, Bird and Tib may not be here for Christmas, after all. Their mama and daddy hope to be sufficiently settled in Dallas to have Christmas there and they are tentatively set to go flying westward the day school is out. So if they are to have a Christmas tree at Sweet Apple, it has to be early.

We went shopping for one the other afternoon since Bird's idea, a homegrown one dug up and potted, seemed beyond my strength and Tib's idea, a shining aluminum one, struck horror to my old-fashioned heart.

The first place had a strange stock of limp trees that appeared to have expired and then been dyed. By unanimous decision we left them. The second place had more balsams than anything else and I used my remaining strength to resist them, holding out for a scrawny but real down-home type Scotch pine.

After that it was complete capitulation. They wanted lights. We bought three strings. They wanted tinsel. We got 12 yards. They wanted to put up the tree and start decorating it the minute we walked in the house. That's what we did.

The enthusiasm for the tree and our old tacky, hand-me-down angel dissipated any lingering opposition I had to an early, store-bought, electric lighted tree.

Every time one of them backed off and surveyed our work with shining eyes and murmured that it was "the mos' beau-full tree in the world." I found myself agreeing wholeheartedly. Then we plugged in the lights!

How was I to know the strings of lights I bought were the BLINKING kind? The darned things go on and off as frantically as a motel "vacancy" sign. Just to look at them gave me spots before my eyes and a bad case of the jitters.

A friend called up and I wailed to her that we had a nervous, fidgety, twitching Christmas tree and she volunteered her husband's help in gentling it down. But I don't know, maybe we'll let it be. Bird and Tib love it. In addition to being "mos' beau-full," it now does something, which is more than you can say for any other Christmas tree we ever had.

The 1974 kidnapping of Atlanta Constitution editor Reg Murphy shocked the nation. After a harrowing experience, the editor was ransomed by Managing Editor Jim Minter. Murphy's kidnapper eventually served a long prison term. During the ordeal, Sibley went to the Murphy home in Atlanta to help comfort the editor's wife. FBI agents were present. "I dictated this column from a nearby drugstore," Sibley recalls. "I didn't want to tie up the phones at home. When I left, I asked Virginia (Murphy) if there was anything I could bring. 'Yes,' she said. 'Toilet paper.' With all those people in the house, she needed it."

Feb. 25, 1974
Kindness helps fill the void

- - - - -

No family is ever ready for a catastrophe and a kidnapping must rank as one of the worst things that ever happend to any family. But the touching and warming thing to me is how public sympathy and the small, quiet, standby services of friends seem to rise up to fill the void created by fear and anxiety and loneliness.

All of us see this in time of death, of course, and saw it last week at the home of Reg and Virginia Murphy, the day after the *Constitution* editor was kidnapped. That first day after he disappeared there had been no word and nobody knew what to hope for or what exactly to fear. The terrible uncertainty and the dragging, oppressive weariness were all that most of those who waited had to keep us company as the hours passed. The exception, of course, was the cheerful little stir created in the house by those who came to "just be here in case we can help."

Neighbors, friends from the church and members of Virginia's garden club rallied 'round. Some of the husbands came and stayed to do the tasks that men do best — light a fire on the hearth and keep it replen-ished with wood from the backyard, answer the door in case of unwel-come intrusion and just be there if a strong arm or a broad shoulder were needed in the night. But most of the people who came were young women, pretty young women with children to pick up at school later and husbands that must be called around suppertime. They came in their

REG MURPHY, EDITOR OF *THE CONSTITUTION*

pretty frocks or their slacks and sneakers and they headed swiftly and unerringly for the kitchen. There the smell of fresh-made coffee filled the air. Somebody scrambled eggs and made toast and persuaded Virginia to pause a moment in the breakfast room and eat a little. They washed dishes and checked out the refrigerator and the cupboards and vanished out the backdoor to return a little later with arms loaded with grocery bags.

"Those photographers!" one of them sniffed good humoredly about the cameramen at the door. "So busy taking pictures when they could have offered to help us with these bags."

The bags contained coffee, bottles of soft drinks, delicatessen potato salad and quantities of paper cups. One husband went home for a big coffee pot and somebody brought ice. Covered dishes began to arrive at front door and back. Many friends were terribly conscious that the presence of one more person in the house might be a burden but they wanted to do something so they rang the doorbell and handed in a foil wrapped dish or a box, saying simply, "There's a card inside" and disappeared. I saw some of these offerings as they were opened and they spelled hours of loving, thoughtful work. Seemingly all over the city women had cancelled their plans for the afternoon and stayed home to bake cookies or a cake, to fry chicken or make a congealed salad. One woman had persuaded her grocer to open early and had bought and baked a ham.

In the dining room the table was spread and food set out and replenished as it ran low. Through it all the girls in the kitchen chatted cheerfully, never allowing themselves the luxury of long silences or talk about what might be happening. If they could stop Virginia as she wandered through they would give her a brief hug and urge her to sleep or eat. Or they would hand out cookies and soft drinks to the youngsters who came to be with the Murphys' daughters and sometimes grab a passing child and hug her hard — as if the force of love itself, as if food and drink and keeping the household going might be a bulwark against disaster.

"What's it like? What's it like to live and work and raise a family in the South or anywhere? Fun and rewarding and exasperating and heartbreaking and frustrating, sometimes ranging all the way from exciting to comfortable." As for her early days as a pioneering female reporter, Sibley writes, "I make no pretense that females had what we've since come to call equal opportunity."

April 18, 1975
Analyzing Southern women

- - - - -

A correspondent who does a spot of freelance writing now and then is attempting to put together a book about what it's like to be a woman in the South. He has propounded the question to me and, as a result, given me a bad day or two. I am like one of those eyewitnesses reporters are always interviewing. I just looked dazed and say, "Glugg!"

If you're in the crash or fire or whatever, you've been too busy coping to get the larger view of the whole situation. If you've been a woman in the South all your life you are too close to the thing to have a useful perspective. You know how it has been with you and some other women you've known well but there are millions of women who have had a different hold of things, different experiences and different reactions. What's it like? What's it like to live and work and raise a family in the South or anywhere? Fun and rewarding and exasperating and heartbreaking and frustrating, sometimes ranging all the way from exciting to comfortable.

The writer, a college professor, is presumably going to ask a lot of women in various fields the same questions and pool the results. I am sure if any of you reading this feel disposed to give him a hand with your experiences he'll be most grateful.

My experience as a working woman in the South has been happy. I have been fortunate to do work that I enjoyed for people I liked and respected. Not all women I know have been so lucky, but a great many of them have.

When I got my first newspaper job, a high schooler working on Saturdays and vacations in that very southern city, Mobile, Ala., I met all kinds of women in positions of importance and influence. One of my

MARGARET MITCHELL

first murder trial acquaintances was a woman lawyer, Miss Rosa Gerhart. My first social worker was a brilliant and charming woman of great culture and matching patience and tolerance — Miss Florence Van Sickler.

Two newspaper reporters whose skill and experience I admired and sometimes drew on were women, Frances Durham and Kathleen Randolph. Mrs. Durham had covered police in New Orleans at a turbulent time in history when things were so bad she said her city editor offered to give her a ball of twine to unwind, Hansel and Gretel fashion, so he could track her down if she disappeared.

There were many more men lawyers and many more men newspaper reporters, of course, and I make no pretense that females had what we've since come to call equal opportunity. Generally, women lawyers handled domestic relations cases and women reporters were content to be assigned to church and fraternal organizations, if not the tea-party and wedding stuff. I suppose they could have run for office. After all, about that time Alabama had, briefly, a woman governor, Mrs. Dixie Graves.

In all the years I have been in Atlanta I have seen many women in effective positions of leadership in the community. There are more now, of course, and there will be more in the future but I doubt if Atlanta women have ever been meek, self-effacing types. Wasn't Eleanor Raoul Green one of the country's best fighters for the right to vote? I thought of her the other day when a reporter in North Carolina told me his wife uses her maiden name — not just at work as I've always done, but on the deed to the house they bought, in the telephone directory and even at parties when they are introduced as Mr. and Miss — to the general confusion of other guests. He mentioned this with pride, as if she were some kind of revolutionary.

I believe Mrs. Green was calling herself Eleanor Raoul 40 or 50 years ago. And how about that other dainty flower of the Old South, Margaret Mitchell? She not only wrote one of the world's best-selling books for all time, she shocked her parents' friends back in the pre-book days by having her name, Miss Mitchell, alongside that of her husband, John Marsh, on their mailbox.

Somehow — and I can't document this — I have a feeling that being a woman in the South is about what it is to be a woman anywhere. Or, for that matter, a person anywhere.

"I was so proud of Rosalynn Carter," Sibley recalls. "President Carter had said his wife didn't support the ERA, but (at this luncheon) she said he was wrong, and she wore a badge that day showing her support for the amendment." But the simple statement of women's rights has never been ratified. "I think it's terrible that it hasn't been," Sibley says.

Jan. 3, 1977
It's time for ERA

- - - - -

The passage of the Equal Rights Amendment for women doesn't seem as hopeless this year as it has in years past. There's actually a movement afoot in the Georgia legislature to launch an all-out effort to win passage of the ERA. You could have knocked me over with a hoecake when I learned that the other day.

Word came in an invitation from Georgia Senate leaders to a luncheon meeting Monday in the Garden Room across from the state capitol.

Sen. Peter Banks of Barnesville, Senate majority leader John R. Riley of Savannah and Sen. Pierre Howard of Decatur will be the hosts, and look at the "name" women who have been invited to appear:

Rosalynn Carter, soon to be the nation's First Lady; Mary Beth Busbee, Georgia's First Lady; Betty Talmadge, wife (until their divorce is granted) of U.S. Sen. Herman Talmadge; Colleen Nunn, wife of U.S. Sen. Sam Nunn; and Shirley Miller, wife of Lt. Gov. Zell Miller are all said to be supporters of the ERA, and all have been invited to the luncheon meeting.

Sen. Banks said the purpose of the meeting was to let other members of the Senate know that there is growing sentiment for the ERA and to rally support for its passage in both the Senate and the House in January.

Things looked so bad for the amendment in the General Assembly last year that women's groups pushing for it joined forces and asked that it be tabled for the session. (I don't think the poor outlook was totally due to the fact that women who oppose the ERA serve lunch to the legislators on Valentine's Day. The assumption here is that all the good cooks, the true homebodies, are in the "anti" group — a fallacious assumption, needless to say. Some highly domesticated women with formidable kitchen skills favor the broad and liberal provisions of the ERA.)

What nobody ever tells the women who oppose the ERA is that in

ROSALYNN CARTER

spite of the Supreme Court equal rights ruling, enforcement is very spotty. Some women get paid the same as their male counterparts — at last — but everybody knows women who are doing a good job and are denied promotions they deserve on one pretext or another but simply because they are women.

Betty Talmadge has long been incensed over the unfair treatment received by a capable young woman she knows, passed over repeatedly for promotion in state government. This young woman was widowed a few years back, left with small children, a horrendous pile of bills and no qualifications for earning money. She struggled with poor-paying jobs, sending herself to school, and finally landed a job in state government where, by all accounts, she has been able and effective. But never promoted.

Maybe the ERA wouldn't change all of that, but it will formalize legal equality and open up the way.

The Stop ERA crowd professes to believe that women have it better now than they'd ever have it under the ERA, that we are protected and looked after. It's the same argument we used to hear against civil rights. The same argument, really, that flourished to protect the institution of slavery.

Maybe with the Senate in there pitching, the ERA will make it this time after two ignominious defeats. It's high time.

On the bitter cold day that a Georgian became president, Jimmy and Rosalynn Carter got out of their official car and walked the parade route along Pennsylvania Avenue. Sibley walked right alongside, sticking to the sidewalk. "When they got to the White House, Rosalynn told me later, it was so cold that she asked if she could turn up the thermostat. But he told her, 'No, put on another sweater.'"

Jan. 20, 1977
Jimmy Carter will be inaugurated today

- - - - -

"The inauguration of the President of the United States is a solemn ritual in which a simple 35-word oath of office elevates a citizen to awesome power and responsibility. It is an achievement of peaceful transition and continuity through change, the climax of a process whereby a free people select one of themselves to be their Chief Magistrate for the next four years."

Those words are from the souvenir program issued four years ago on the eve of the inauguration of Richard M. Nixon.

It's scary when you read that neat, dignified little "Inaugural Guide" with its dark blue cover and gold seal and realize how it all turned out. There are pictures of Nixon and Spiro Agnew with a quote from Nixon's victory statement on election night. There are lists of inaugural events and committees and a map showing the route of parade from the oath-taking site in front of the Capitol to the White House.

It is festive but with tremendous dignity — a full sense of the historic implications of the inaugural, a full appreciation of "the happy morning" of America's existence in the world of nations and the importance of the will of the people who name a president.

Those people working so hard to see that it was a proper inaugural, a gala one but fitting and memorable, must have been just as full of hope as the weary, excited, confused young people who will see today's inauguration of Georgian Jimmy Carter to fruition.

You wonder where they are now, those inaugural planners and pushers of four years ago. Are they as exiled as the men they inaugurated?

JIMMY CARTER

How will this one turn out? Four years from now will it have been such a constructive, nationally satisfying four years that the same group will be back burning the midnight oil, eating canned stew, putting circles under their eyes setting up a re-run, another Jimmy Carter inauguration?

Historians may be the only really contented people in the world. They have the detachment, the objectivity to rise above the fireworks display, the shuffle and push to get to the balls, the concerts, the "better" parties, the parades and festivals.

They get the long view of inauguration and eventually they will put this one in the proper slot, along with that of Thomas Jefferson and Rutherford B. Hayes, of James Polk and Grover Cleveland and Harry S. Truman.

Unfortunately, it can't be classed with the inaugural of that other Southerner, Woodrow Wilson, because that ascetic gentleman from Virginia — AND Georgia — felt that the festive air of a ball "jarred the solemnity of an inauguration" launching an era which lasted all through the '20s.

The next inaugural ball honored Franklin D. Roosevelt in 1933 but then, because of the Depression and the Second World War, they started skipping them until Harry S. Truman, that piano-playing president who loved a good caper, revived them in 1949.

Maybe it's something Presbyterian in me that makes me inclined to the view of that joyless Presbyterian president, Woodrow Wilson — that the oath of office is the thing, the big and moving moment when the earth must pause a fraction of a second on its axis to catch its breath because of the importance of the occasion.

The faces of millions of Americans must be turned toward Washington, waiting and listening and praying that this time, this one will lead us well.

Goodness knows, the oath itself is not a thing of poetic beauty. Its plain words are pretty much the same as the ones said by justices of the peace and legislative pages when they assume their duties. But I can't help it, they move me, and I am looking forward to hearing Jimmy Carter today when he places his hand on the Bible and says: "I do solemnly swear that I will faithfully execute the Office of President of the United States, and will to the best of my ability, preserve, protect and defend the Constitution of the United States."

Her mother, Evelyn Barber Sibley of Alford, Fla., was "Muv" to Constitution readers. She was the subject of numerous Sibley columns in The Constitution. *"Harold Martin (her fellow columnist) wrote that Muv was 'the eternal matriarch, merry and wise,'" Sibley says. "I liked that."*

June 29, 1978
Making an absence easier

- - - - -

My mother called that morning and said the pain in her chest had come back, even worse than the first time six or seven weeks before. She agreed, at my insistence, that she "might" let her next-door neighbor, who was standing by, take her to the hospital later, if she felt like it. I said I was on my way but it would take me six hours to get there and she'd better go on to the doctor.

"I might," she said, "and I might not."

There was a crowd in Muv's yard and on her porch when my son and I drove up to her front gate. She had died in her sleep an hour earlier.

Part of the pain of grief and loss is always, I suppose, guilt. I should have been there, I thought. If I had only hurried. If we hadn't stopped for a cup of coffee or to call from Columbus.... if... if...

At such times friends and neighbors are a family's strength. They told us we were not at fault. They said Muv valued her privacy and, most of all, her independence, that she would have elected to depart this earth by herself and with no to-do. She had, they assured us, gone to a fairer land. The minister spoke later of our joining her in "glory," and I wondered what use Muv would have for living in "glory," she who thought Paris, France, looked just like Dothan, Alabama.

Now a little time has gone by. Friends everywhere have cheered and comforted us with their notes and their calls. (Muv would be astonished, I think, at how much mail her death evoked and very touched and pleased at the affection expressed.)

As a family we are, I hope, done with tears — but not with laughter. So much of our time with Muv has been filled with laughter it was hard even as we coped with the horrid details of getting a grave dug and picking out a coffin not to lean together and laugh at something Muv had said or done on such an occasion.

EVELYN SIBLEY

"Do you remember?" we said to one another over and over again. Old friends from Muv's young girlhood came and sat on the porch and set us laughing again at stories of her capers.

"Did you know she was a terrific buck dancer?" one asked.

"Well, I knew she loved to dance," I said, "but I didn't know she could buck dance."

"Oh, honey, she was GOOD!" said the old friend. "Why, I remember...."

I think it was after her cousin's funeral..." And she was off on another story.

She had been our conscience for so many years and our mentor on the rules of behavior, particularly in Alford where there was always danger we would disgrace her, that we found ourselves trying very hard to abide by her rules. There were lapses. Seized by restlessness, I washed a load of clothes, and so it turned out that we had laundry on the line on the day of Muv's funeral. Everybody agreed that Muv would have been mortified in front of her neighbors.

My daughter Mary arrived in such a rush she didn't have enough clothes, and I looked in Muv's closet and pulled out the dress I had sent her for Easter. She had professed to love its bright colors at the time, but I knew she had never put it on and that she really regarded it as too youthful looking for her 83 years.

"I'll wear it a little while — maybe just to the funeral home," Mary said dubiously. "Muv might not like for me — well, can't you just hear her saying, 'May-ree, take that dress off and HANG IT UP!'?"

We could hear that and many more admonitions, and, I suppose, we always will. I hope so because it will make her absence easier.

A reader's telephone call reflected the city's darkened mood as police raced to solve the Missing and Murdered cases, when 27 chidren were abducted and killed. In the midst of the gloom and pessimism, Sibley profiled three Atlantans who were working to promote harmony.

Feb. 22, 1981
The terror that walks our city

- - - - -

"The people of Atlanta make me sick," the woman said over the telephone. "All this killing reflects a sickness in the whole population — the way those concentration camps reflected something rotten in the German people during World War II. I can't wait to get back to California. If my husband can't get transferred I'm going anyhow! How can you stand this place?"

She didn't wait for my answer and I am sorry because I could have told her. The terror that walks our street is something that every Atlanta citizen abhors and is revolted by. It is no more typical of our town than killers anywhere — New York, Boston or her beloved California.

The terrible loss of children has generated something which is almost worse than death and that's the fear which is necessarily infecting other children. I heard the other day about a bold, invincible little 15-year-old black boy who has worked hard to help his "awn-tee" rear a big family of children. He was the friend of the neighborhood and he did odd jobs for everybody. Now he is afraid — afraid to leave the house, afraid to speak to people who used to be his friends. At 15 years a shrewd and industrious little entrepreneur has been broken.

Sure, it's terrible and Atlantans hate it with all their hearts. But there are still reasons to "stand this place," as my caller put it. I heard about three of them from Dorothy Lara-Brand of the Christian Council of Metropolitan Atlanta.

On the first Saturday in March the council is going to hold its annual community breakfast and present special awards to three citizens who make you proud to be an Atlantan.

They are: Frances Pauley, 75, founder of the Georgia Poverty Rights Organization and a familiar figure in the Georgia Legislature, where, it is said, her causes are not always popular but she is admired as "a lover and respector of people"; Alice Browner, who for two years has run "Help House" at 830 Boulevard, emergency housing for homeless and displaced people; Bill Bolling, 33, director of street ministries for St. Luke's Episcopal Church, and founder of the Atlanta Community Food Bank which was launched to receive still edible food donated by restaurants, grocery stores and shippers and move it on to more than 70 on-site feeding institutions.

Each of these people has accomplished the award-winning work while also busy at something else. Originally just a "concerned churchwoman," Frances Pauley has worked with every agency and office having to do with human rights — "a crazy optimist," as she herself puts it, who once said, "I don't think you should ask yourself whether you can do a thing but how it can be done. That starts you out on the right path."

Alice Browner manages to raise money for "Help House" and answer 50 to 60 emergency phone calls per week while working at Economic Opportunity Atlanta and serving on the Atlanta Regional Commission Housing Task Force and the education committee of the Georgia Housing Council. She founded the Decatur Community Council, which is buying the old Scottish Rite Hospital on East Lake Road for a community center.

As director of street ministries for St. Luke's, Bill Bolling also coordinates the soup kitchen there, a free food service which feeds 400 hungry and needy people each day. He talks to those who come in and helps them find jobs and housing and acquaints them with the church's training and counseling center.

Stand this place? the woman asked. How can you help hearing about such citizens as these without a rush of affection and pride in them and in the city in which they toil?

Through Sibley's columns danced a parade of eccentrics over the years — Parsival Cobb, J. Bugger Dowdy, Aunt Dilly, Ms. Peevy, and Francis Brunton, a hobo who lived under the Spring Street viaduct and rode through the downtown streets on a bicycle. "People say I made heroes out of the homeless," Sibley says. "They're not heroes, they're just ordinary people like you and me."

Sept. 1, 1981
Francis Brunton isn't crazy

- - - - -

A man who once offered Francis Brunton a job picking peppers in Middle Georgia called the other day to ask what, if anything, I had heard from the picturesque gentleman who used to ride the streets of Atlanta on his bicycle, selling our newspaper. At the time of his call I had no idea. Minnesota or Washington state, I offered, some foreign place like that.

"You're as crazy as he is," the caller said thoughtfully. "My sister-in-law came from Tacoma and SHE is not the least bit foreign. You admit Francis is crazy, don't you?"

I admit nothing, I said loftily. Francis is unusual, maybe a touch eccentric, interesting, different. But crazy? What a loose word to apply to a gentle, kind and friendly man! The world has become so conformist there's hardly room for people who go their way, behaving in an unconventional, unorthodox fashion. Once, not too many years ago, somebody thought so little of Francis' behavior in Minnesota or perhaps it was the way he was dressed (railroad engineer's cap, jodphurs, baseball socks and shoulder-to-ankle globes and shopping bags) they had him committed to some mental institution. The people who ran the place must not have considered Francis a lunatic because they let him call me and they listened when I gave him a good recommendation.

"Tell them I'm not crazy," Francis implored. "Tell them I don't drink and I'm not dangerous."

So I did and they listened and let him out. He subsequently showed up at the Tacoma, Wash., library and was banned from the stacks for taking along a hot plate and cooking among the books.

Anyhow, the librarian liked him, recognized in him a true book-lover and readmitted him to the sacred precincts of the library as soon as he gave up the hot plate and the groceries. That was almost the last thing I had heard from Francis until the middle Georgia pepper-grower called.

"If I hear from him do you want him to come back and work for you again?" I asked.

"NO!" cried the grower. "He didn't work when he was here. He spent his time reading with a great big magnifying glass and writing stuff nobody understood on the margins of books and papers IN RED!"

"Then... "

"Why am I asking?" he laughed. "I don't know. I just think about the old fellow from time to time. He was nutty but I kind of liked him. My wife and I were talking and I thought you might know."

What I didn't know that day I now know. I think. I had an envelope in the morning mail with Francis' unmistakable red script all over it. I opened it with interest and found a bulletin for the Sunday morning, July 5 service at the Fond du Lac Community Church in Duluth, Minn. The sermon topic that day was "Peter's Restoration." The choir sang "When I Survey the Wondrous Cross" and "Blessed Assurance." There was no comment from Francis. Disappointed, I put down the church program and picked up the envelope.

It was addressed to me and Betsy Meade, Atlanta, Georgia, U.S.A. (Miss Meade, formerly of our staff is now in Egypt with her husband, Donald Hastings Jr., and their two children.) In the corner Francis directed us to please call somebody whose name and telephone number I can't read. But for his old friends like the pepper grower who still think of him and wonder, his address was perfectly clear: "I am at Gerald Eklunds Home 218 AC 626-1090, 13328 West End Street, Duluth, U.S.A., Minnesota."

He would be pleased to hear from old friends and admirers, I know. A card or even a church program would be acceptable.

At 46, Sibley sold her home in midtown Atlanta and moved into a 119-year-old log cabin near Woodstock, 30 miles north of Atlanta. It had been a pioneer home, and later the one-room Sweet Apple School, named for an apple tree in the yard. She made it livable, adding electricity, a bathroom and stairs, and bringing logs from another abandoned cabin to build an "annex" to her home. Through her many columns about Sweet Apple, Atlanta readers exercise their love for nostalgia, and for preserving the past.

June 15, 1986
Real country living over at Sweet Apple
- - - - -

It was one of those mornings when the sun seemed slow to come up, lingering back of the pines on the hill and the big oak tree but filling the interstices with gold. Time enough to wander around the yard barefoot and in my nightgown before traffic on the old dirt road picks up, I thought.

The thicket planted — or maybe accumulated is the word — between the house and the road gives some privacy in the summertime when trees and bushes are well leafed out. Even so, you don't want joggers or the kids on the school bus to catch even a little glimpse of you shoeless and in a ragged shift. So the best plan is to go early.

There are so many things needing checking in even a neglected, weedy patch like mine. Where you've made a start, made a new bed, dug out weeds, thinned or transplanted wouldn't set a real gardener's pulses hammering. But for some of us, a little progress is a lovesome thing. And you do want to get out early and see what the night has brought to your domain.

What it brought to my domain was the sound of a bulldozer cranking up in the woods across the road. And that was joined by the whine of power saws. We knew it was coming. The surveyor's crews were over there hammering in stakes and tying red ribbons to them weeks ago. And a man at the grocery store up at the crossroads said he heard the plan was to build 65 houses — or was it 165? — on our road. But being a cockeyed optimist, as the song has it, I didn't quite believe it would happen.

A bulldozer and a power saw tell me differently. They're coming. They're really coming. They'll want the road paved. They'll want street lights. They'll cut down trees and probably plant lawns and old Sweet Apple cabin will be the sole survivor of country living as it used

to be. The notion was so depressing, I started to go back in the house and put on my shoes and go to town. But I was waylaid by the little triangle where I planted wormwood and six wonderful catnip plants which Lawrence Coleman, grandson of our old-time neighbor, Mrs. Crow, brought me. I am determined to keep those catnip plants going because Lawrence and his wife, Kathryn, firmly believe that they are descendants of the original crop at Sweet Apple, preserved by Mrs. Crow and her daughter, Christine.

It's sort of a defiant gesture toward suburbia to try to preserve the old Sweet Apple catnip, I guess. Mrs. Crow said it was once "the saving of the settlement," but doctors and drugstores have moved in all around us. And who needs catnip any more? Still I pushed some more dirt around their roots and patted it and went on to pull a curled leaf off the little sweetheart rose bush. My new neighbors across the street, not a road, will probably shame me with real rose gardens instead of a few random bushes stuck here and there in the yard. They may even go in for poison sprays so their rose leaves won't curl and their phlox won't come down with mildew.

It's going to be all right, I tell myself as I check the morning glories I planted as a further screen against the road. People have to live somewhere and my late neighbor, Olivia Johnson, would have welcomed a whole settlement of new houses. She walked down the road to welcome us, saying, "I'm so proud to have new neighbors."

It's the proper attitude. There was something said at church a week or so ago about loving your neighbor. I've been acquainted with that stricture all my life but, funny thing, I never realized it applied to strangers moving next door and across the road. And yet we haven't had any neighbors we haven't liked.

Maybe it's the end of real country living I'm bemoaning. Most of the neighbors we had when we moved to Sweet Apple are gone and so are their houses and barns. We no longer hear gee-haw directions to a mule plowing a cornfield or are awakened by a rooster's crowing. The creak of a windlass in the well is no more and I bet there isn't a milk cow or a billy goat or a privy within 20 miles. And it happened so fast.

If you're about to live in the midst of suburbia, maybe you better start getting ready for it. The first thing I decided to do is put on my clothes and shoes before I hit the yard from now on.

Traditionalist she is, and yet an iconoclast, too. After first scolding a newcomer to the city for criticizing Atlantans' preoccupation with the lost cause of the War Between the States, she then wrote this column rebuking what she called "tedious professional Southerners."

March 28, 1983
The war is over

- - - - -

A week ago in a Sunday column I attempted to answer the complaints and rebukes of a gentleman newly come to Atlanta who is offended by our eternal hashing and rehashing of the details of the Civil War. I replied in effect that Atlanta is a near-Yankee Southern city which re-fights the Civil War out of an interest in history, more than out of any hostility toward the descendants of those Union soldiers who have been jokingly characterized as "careless with matches." Even before the war, I pointed out, some valued Atlanta citizens, notably L.P. Grant, a New Englander, were from the North.

Now, it seems that we do a lot more mouthing North-South stuff than I realized. The "Good Ol' Boy" syndrome has been infectious and oth-erwise sensible Atlantans, who only know Northerners to love them, have been guilty of becoming caricature "rebels." Several people have written in to tell me of this silly business. I am surprised and a little bored with these tedious professional Southerners. I bet if you checked into their background, you wouldn't find a Confederate hero on either side of the family.

The excuse Atlantans have for keeping alive the Battle of Atlanta, of course, is that this was the only American city to be conquered and burned. Conquered people, as Europeans will tell you, remember. But by the time rebuilding started, even Gen. William Tecumseh Sherman himself was cordially and hospitably received by Atlantans. They had felt the heat of his fires. They had suffered wounds. They had been burned out of their homes and lost sons and brothers in the battle.

But they adopted the attitude that the war was over and it wasn't all

Sherman's fault anyhow. He came back and Atlantans gave him a party. It's an attitude Americans demonstrated toward Japan and Germany after World War II.

Even the social thing some women complained about is surprising to me. I have never actually known anybody who snooted a neighbor or acquaintance because she happened to be from above the Mason-Dixon line. It may happen. As Satchel Paige expressed it, I'm not much for the "social ramble" anyhow.

The gracious and generous "Old South" people I have known would cut their throats before they would offend an otherwise agreeable visitor or newcomer. I always thought it was the mark of the breed. There was an old Mobilian I used to know — and that, unlike Atlanta, is an Old South city — who instructed her children to be particularly nice to anybody who came from any point north of Mobile County.

"Poor things," she said with real compassion, "they can't help it." Her voice would drop to a whisper. "Not everybody could be born in Mobile."

Scarlett herself was criticized by Melanie for being friends with Yankees. Did that stop her? She wasn't a fool. She knew interesting and resourceful people come from all kinds of places and she especially liked that resourceful bit.

My own mother had a Confederate grandfather who wanted her named Dixie Lee for some kind of fergit-hell reason. Fortunately, saner heads prevailed and she got a name that came out of a book and had nothing whatever to do with the Late Unpleasantness. (Some people on that side of the family persisted in calling her Dixie until she died. A lot of girls her age got that name and she thought it was preferable to Bonnie Blue in any case.)

For those who feel like disadvantaged Atlantans because they came from "off," I am sorry. For those who are bored by the whole North-South commotion, my sympathy. I'm bored by it myself.

Atlanta native Alfred Uhry's moving play became a celebrated motion picture. It provided a glimpse of progressive 1950s Atlanta. "I knew Alfred Uhry's mother," Sibley recalls. "Every Christmas The Constitution used to have 'Ten Opportunities.' The Family Welfare Bureau picked ten families that needed special things at Christmas. Mrs. Uhry and I served together on the board of directors of the Family Welfare Bureau."

March 27, 1990
'Miss Daisy' tugs at Southern hearts

- - - - -

The old shiver of recognition trembled between Atlanta's shoulder blades. The we've-been-there feeling was like fuzzy rabbit tracks on Atlanta backbones.

While the world watched the Academy Awards ceremony, Atlantans, awaiting the fate of a simple little movie called "Driving Miss Daisy," knew it wasn't just a movie.

"Driving Miss Daisy," an artistic triumph for the town of its birth, didn't have to win any awards as far as the home folks were concerned.

It WAS Atlanta and Atlanta people in a time perhaps gone, with attitudes maybe changed but with people real and true and exasperatingly lovesome as everybody's grandma and Aunt Minnie.

The wonder was that Hollywood could even consider for its highest accolade a skinny old lady with thin skimpy hair and a sharp tongue. Or that moviemakers would be cognizant of an aging black man who could out-Tom Uncle Tom when he was of a mind to.

Everybody knows that movies thrive on violence and sex.

"Driving Miss Daisy" had neither, except in the subtlest, almost undefined way, which is the way "nice" Atlantans like the old lady named

Miss Daisy knew about such things in the years between 1948 and 1973.
She knew her beloved Jewish Temple was bombed. She knew Martin
Luther King Jr. had some logic on his side when he fought for rights for
blacks. But she knew these things from a detached, well-cared-for position in a stately Druid Hills home.

She wasn't out there in the thick of conflict, no more than most
Atlantans were. But like nearly all of us claimed, she had feelings.

She considered herself sensitive to pain in other people. And she was,
but she still spoke of black people as "they," just as she sniffed at a

JESSICA TANDY

daughter-in-law who would "socialize with Episcopalians." She still
wouldn't put up with her servants snitching a 33-cent can of salmon
from the pantry or taking the long way around to the Piggly Wiggly.

Gas cost money, and although she had plenty, she remembered well
when her family existed on grits and gravy and she taught at the south
Atlanta school attended by poor boys such as Willie Hartsfield, later
Atlanta Mayor William B. Hartsfield.

Before the Oscars, a couple of dozen moviegoers went to the Tara
Theater for the early matinee of "Driving Miss Daisy" Monday afternoon.
They laughed and murmured among themselves to see such Atlanta

landmarks as Druid Hills in dogwood and azalea season, Euclid Avenue stores and The Temple on Peachtree Street.

Those who had been present at the dinner honoring Martin Luther King Jr. on his return from collecting the Nobel Peace prize in Sweden knew the moviemakers muffed it when they put the party in a white-columned colonial hotel instead of rebuilding the old Dinkler Plaza.

But so what? The speech in the movie was real, taken from tapes. And the feelings of dressed-up Atlantans who sat around the party tables and listened to themselves described as men and women of good will, dangerous only because of their indifference and inaction, were real.

It was an Atlanta attitude at the time, and many Atlantans took it like Miss Daisy, listening and looking at the empty chair beside her where her black servant and best friend, Hoke, should have been sitting if her courage had matched her good will.

Alfred Uhry, the Atlantan who wrote the play and as a boy played at the home where the movie was filmed, grandson to a lady named Miss Lena, knew these things and set them down with infinite skill.

But how did Jessica Tandy, an Englishwoman generally seen on Broadway, know how it was with Atlanta? How did Morgan Freeman, who was born in Mississippi and became a top-flight professional and winner of a score of acting awards, know how a humble black man needing a job could swallow his pride and wait out the whims of a crotchety old woman in 1948? Granting that they are superlative actors, there's a possibility that Atlanta's truth is universal, experienced by people everywhere who face the confusion of change, fighting with threadbare pride to preserve their own way of life and the independence that is no longer possible.

Miss Daisy offers a lesson, surrendering at last in pain and a moving, contradictory kind of love.

"Miss Daisy" is not another "Gone With the Wind." It's what they call a quiet little picture — quiet like lightning in a summer sky, like a blow to the heart or, as Christopher Morley once put it in defining a human being, like the spark a key makes when it finds the lock it fits.

Could Scarlett O'Hara have done as well in bifocals and drooping chin?

"When I was growing up in Mobile, Ala., we would buy the Sunday Atlanta Constitution *to read Ralph McGill. My father liked the paper so much that he would have died if I hadn't gotten to work for it." In the Nineties, Sibley was surprised to find that the memory of her great editor and mentor was fading, and it troubled her.*

July 23, 1990
The McGill legacy

- - - - -

Years ago a friend of mine picked up a saying in a hospital labor room that has served many of us, her friends, well with the passage of time. A weary countrywoman who was having her fifth or sixth child sweated and thrashed about and groaned, and when the going got particularly rough, she cried, "Lord, Lord, how you fergit!" It no longer has a labor-room connotation for us. Whatever the recurring pain is, we say to one another, "Lord, Lord, how you fergit!" The latest example of fergitfulness to come my way concerns my late boss and Georgia's late distinguished editor-publisher Ralph McGill.

Virginia Hooks of Decatur writes that she cannot find any information about Mr. McGill.

"I am in my 50s now, and I learned to read a newspaper very young by reading his column daily. He wrote such great articles. . . . I would like to find some of them now."

So far, so good. But Ms. Hooks said she could not find any books about Mr. McGill, and she called this newspaper, talking to three people who told her they had not heard of him. Before the shock wore off, I was muttering, "Lord, Lord, how you fergit!" Having just come from a meeting at which 43 applications for Ralph McGill journalism scholarships were considered, it seemed to me that even the young, who had not been born when he died in 1969, have a reverent regard for our editor. And the grown-ups who were there to pick the scholarship winners certainly brought him to jolly, incandescent life with their stories about him.

But if it's true, as Ms. Hooks says, that there's a vast area of ignorance

RALPH MCGILL

about Mr. McGill, I hasten to give the information-seekers what help I can. First, Mr. McGill's son, Ralph Jr., and his widow, Dr. Mary Lynn Morgan, are alive and well in Atlanta and can provide firsthand information. Then there's Harold Martin's fine book *Ralph McGill, Reporter*. I saw several copies in the biography section of the downtown library.

For serious researchers, Emory University Library has a prodigious McGill collection. The Atlanta Historical Society also has a valuable McGill file. Then there are the books Mr. McGill himself wrote, *The*

South and the Southerner and *The Fleas Come With the Dog* for a start.

And for those in our building who are too new to the business to know, Mr. McGill wrote for *The Constitution* for three decades, was high in the counsels of the mighty both nationally and internationally and was a warm and friendly and very brave man. He was in the forefront of fighters for civil rights and, as a woman once told me, did the thinking for a lot of Southerners who had not got around to thinking. I re-read Harold Martin's book about him every year or so, and it's not a bad idea for Ms. Hooks and others who want to understand our region and one of the good men who helped shape it.

An article in the paper described how moonlight would assist U.S. fighters and bombers in the Persian Gulf. Thinking about that as she commuted home, Sibley penned this moving description of Atlantans aboard a MARTA train, a bus, and at home as a war began faraway. Her career had started during World War II and commenced through Korea, Vietnam and the Gulf War. "I've seen a heap of war, haven't I?," she says.

Oct. 17, 1990
New moons are for bombers

- - - - -

New moons are for lovers. New moons are for children to wish on. New moons are for bombers.

Except for that slender horn of silver in the sky, the night was dark, and the scant crowd of after-hour bus travelers, hurrying across the damp concourse of the Lenox MARTA station, talked about it a bit. The old "bomber's moon" of World War II years, one passenger said, was outdated by new equipment. "Our boys," he said, looking out the bus window, "would need it tonight."

"They won't go tonight," another offered. "It will be Friday at least."

"I hope they'll never go," a woman said.

We all sighed restively and spoke of supper. The bus started, and one woman took out some embroidery, others picked up newspapers and books, and the heads of the others bobbled in sleep.

Near Roswell, our destination, a foreign-speaking woman, probably French, rushed to the driver and urgently asked directions to a certain dress shop.

A male passenger, rousing, said it was across the highway bridge some distance but he was going that way and could give her a ride. She shook her head emphatically, spoke some French and stepped out into the darkness.

We smiled at one another in weary communion. We knew he meant well.

There was no harm in him.

Moments later, though, those of us who went straight home walked into harm — the most harm that can befall our planet: a war.

My family rushed to meet me, and over their heads I heard from a TV just brought into the kitchen the word: "The liberation of Kuwait has begun."

The spaghetti simmered on the stove. The children collected around the kitchen table, intent on food, homework and a letter they were writing. The adults couldn't move.

We stood there and listened. So much of it was talk and more talk.

It was hard to sort out what half-a-dozen war correspondents in Baghdad were saying. And then we heard the explosions. They spoke of "flashes of light like a million fireflies," borrowing a peaceful country simile.

As they talked, we heard the planes going over and the distant boom of guns. We would be hearing thunder hour after hour, perhaps day after day, one correspondent promised us. Iraqi jet fighters had not gotten off the ground, and when they did, they would be so pocked by bombs from U.S. bombers that they couldn't defend themselves.

"Gentlemen, we are seeing an example of surgical bombing," a broadcaster said lyrically.

Another contradicted him. It wasn't that neat and precise, he contended. A state of emergency had been declared in Israel, and the people there were advised to open their little kits containing gas masks in case the Iraqis came as they had promised with poison gas. Refineries had been hit in Baghdad, one said.

"This is quite something," an English voice in Baghdad said in unintentional understatement.

Walter Cronkite came on and talked about "the scenario" given the world by the U.S. strike: some things were working out as planned, some were "knocked down."

And then he added soberly, "There are Americans dying at this hour." The children finished their spaghetti and opened their books. The 10-year-old resumed work on a letter they want to send to someone they know who went to Saudi Arabia to fight.

"I know it is probably hard," he wrote. "You are very brave."

Outside, the night was very dark, the new moon obscured by clouds.

A glow of optimism filled Atlanta at the start of a new year, and as the Atlanta Olympics loomed ahead, the irrepressible Sibley, and photographer Joey Ivansco, soared over the city in a helicopter. "I didn't know what I was going to write about," she recalls. She went to the paper and penned this love letter to her town.

Dec. 31, 1991
A golden city!

- - - - -

It's my town. I have loved it for 50 years.

Since I first set foot on Peachtree Street, since a young city editor named Lee Rogers steered me toward a typewriter in an old Victorian building at the corner of Alabama and Forsyth Streets, since the first audacious, outrageous Georgia politician said mischievously, "Welcome to the USA! You ain't American till Atlanta has naturalized you."

I have loved its heartbeat — the trains, the factory whistles, the winged traffic in its sky, the jackhammer beat of eternally tearing up and rebuilding. I know its smells of yore, the taste and feel of its weather and some of the valor and heartbreak and folly of its history.

Oh, I love Atlanta. And I thought I knew it. I thought its size and shape were as familiar to me as her child's growing arms and legs are to a mother. I know headstones in its cemeteries, the secret bloom of violets in its alleys, the bridal whiteness of its dogwood in the spring, a forgotten peach tree lifting fragile pink blooms in a junkyard. I know and shrink a little from the prophecies of a wild-eyed evangelist in the park, the easy, offhand way its multimillionaires launch new enterprises, erect cities within cities.

I love its church bells, the gospel sings, the oratory of preachers and politicians. I love the beggar on the corner who receives a paltry coin and, doffing his frayed knitted cap ceremoniously, calls after you: "May goodness and mercy follow you all the days of your life!" I love Atlanta. That's irrefutable.

But KNOW it? That's presumption and delusion.

I went with our photographer, Joey Ivansco, in a helicopter piloted by Paul Paskert to take a New Year's look at my town at sunset.

From the sky it spread before me in cubes and towers and stadium circles and great green swatches of trees and concrete ribbons of expressways.

And I knew it not.

Like Ruth in the land of Boaz, I "stood amid the alien corn."

My large and wise and faulty city, towering into the blue secrets of the late-day sky, had thrust up skyscrapers when I wasn't looking, had diminished the old and familiar. The gold-domed Capitol looked as small as a child's play-pretty. Housing projects were building blocks of a toy village, Grant Field an infinitesimal circlet of green. MARTA stations were cut out by cookie cutters, the Carter presidential library and museum a scattering of pancake-shaped discs. Even mammoth Grady Hospital was dwarfed and dingy.

The buildings that had awed me with their beauty, their stateliness, not long ago — the chaste marble Candler and Hurt and Healey buildings, the banking fortresses of Five Points — lay in a kind of twilight, passed over by the copper-and-gold glory of the setting sun. The sun swept over them to encompass taller, newer buildings in radiance.

What are all these big buildings? I asked my companions that afternoon and again later. Nobody knew all of them. Everybody knew some of them, and together we studied Joey's pictorial tapestry of growth and architectural grandeur, reciting a left-to-right litany: "IBM, First National Bank, AT&T, Southern Bell, Citizens & Southern, Westin Peachtree, Peachtree Center, Georgia-Pacific, 191 Peachtree Towers. . . ." And then as the light turned its old windows to diamonds, "the Hurt Building, Marriott Hotel, the Capitol." At the bottom of the picture, looking strangely small: The Fulton Courthouse, City Hall, the Candler Building and the soap-bar rectangles of state office buildings, one of them whimsically called the Sloppy building after the nickname of the late longtime state Rep. James Floyd.

"Thought you knew Atlanta," one of my co-workers gibed later, and I had to explain. Atlanta isn't all-knowable. Atlanta, now in 1992 entering its 155th year, is as cities go a young and growing place, full of capricious and notional ways. It adores building; it flourishes on change. Some of those buildings, the Citizens & Southern tower, for one, will have a new name by Wednesday — NationsBank. Even the names of streets are changed from time to time to keep old-timers off-balance. The city enters the New Year happily on the wings of the "wild chase of time."

Visible and tangible here in the lambent light of the setting winter sun, Atlanta makes a picture worth the keeping. And it reverses the cliche that to know is to love. Some of us love the unknowableness of it.

Through the crowds and the lines of security barriers, Sibley reached the office on the day after Centennial Olympic Park had been bombed. A madman's act had perhaps marred forever the memory of the city's greatest moment. In her 55th year of writing for the paper, Sibley contributed this column to the Atlanta Games Olympic coverage. "I wouldn't have missed it," she says. "To sit out anything as major as a story like that... Being a reporter is the highest calling. You do the people a service, you let the people know. I think that's major."

July 28, 1996
Tears are the only reaction that makes sense
- - - - -

You're useless if you cry, I have heard them tell welfare workers and soldiers. But what else can you do when a senseless, vicious act of terrorism happens to innocent, fun-loving young people a block from where you work? How can you not cry for the dead and the wounded and for your hometown, which has tried so hard to make it the best Olympics ever? So I cried while I called the office and dressed and started the car.

It seemed that the very heavens wept with us. A slow, gray rain started in the green aisles of the expressway and gathered force as I got closer to town.

Traffic was so light that I knew fearful people must be staying at home and those in cars to the right and the left looked gray-faced and tense and I knew they were listening to the news of the park bombing on their radios.

The old question — "why?" — was uppermost in my mind. Why did it happen to those hundreds on the TWA plane over Long Island? Why did it happen to our cheerful, gala, peace-loving town? A lot full of merry, colorful tents on Edgewood Avenue looked lonely and bleak. The tents flapped drearily in the rain. The sign advertising "Cold Ice Water" seemed soggy and ready to collapse. There were no vendors and no customers.

A little closer to Five Points there were small clumps of people in makeshift plastic raincoats. Three teenage boys had our newspaper with the headline, "Explosion Rocks Centennial Park," spread before them. They had come to town to have fun but what was this? Danger? The policeman at the corner who directed me around a barrier said there still might be danger. He seemed philosophical about it. There's always danger, he seemed to be saying. And I suppose there is.

In the office, past the security guards, whose jobs now seem more relevant than I ever imagined, reporters and editors worked silently.

There were no tears but no smiles either.

The older ones, like me, had been through catastrophic assignments before. We didn't talk about it but I think some of us remember the Paris crash, which killed a planeload of our citizens, the Winecoff hotel fire which took a toll of 109 people, the death of the Rev. Martin Luther King Jr., the assassination of President John Kennedy and later his brother Robert. Grief and pain and death are out there waiting for a lot of us.

The instinct of all of us is to check on our own. Are they safe? Did the teenage boys who love music go to that concert which poured 50,000 young people into the park just before the bomb exploded? Happily they were at home asleep. My big grandson, who is a news photographer, was there, I knew. Wasn't he always where news was breaking? He had 13 stitches in his scalp to show for the violence at Clark Atlanta University a few years ago. I called his house and found he got home from covering one of the Olympic events, fell into bed but did not sleep before he was called and dispatched to the scene of the bombing. He ran out of the house putting on his clothes as he went. If he were in any danger, his wife told me, it was the danger of falling asleep in his tracks. Somehow I wouldn't have believed that it was a danger Atlanta has earned.

Our town has not been asleep where security is concerned. We have been so vigilant those of us who have always felt safe in Atlanta, even by dark of night, may have scoffed a little at the stringent measures that have been imposed with the Olympics. The officers who spotted the bomb and started clearing the area before it went off, thereby saving many lives, proved that care has been taken. Atlanta has taken care, we do care.

INDEX

FURMAN BISHER is in his 48th year as a lead sports columnist for the Atlanta papers.

A tireless and prolific observer of the sports scene, he writes four columns a week for the *Journal-Constitution*, though he may write daily if the event he is covering merits it. That could be somewhere in Georgia, or on the other side of the continent, or in Europe.

He was born Nov. 4, 1918 on a farm near Denton, N.C., near Charlotte. A detail of his youth that survives from an early corporate bio is that he once won a cow-milking contest.

Furman was a student at Furman University in 1934-36; that his and the school's names are the same is a coincidence. He transferred to, and graduated from, the University of North Carolina with an A.B. in journalism in 1938.

Bisher was editor of the Lumberton, N.C., *Voice* in 1938-39; reporter for the High Point, N.C., *Enterprise* in 1939-40; and a reporter, religion editor, state editor and sports makeup editor for the *Charlotte News* in 1940-43. During World War II, he served for three years as a lieutenant senior grade in the Navy in air operations on Pearl Harbor and Midway Island, and at Pensacola. "I was never shot at, and never shot at anyone," he says.

Returning to the *News* in 1946, he turned to the field of sportswriting and was named *News* sports editor in '48. "It took that long for vacancies to occur and for me to get in there," he recalls.

Moving to the city with which his work would become synonymous, he joined *The Atlanta Constitution* as sports editor in 1950, and moved to *The Atlanta Journal* in the same role in 1957.

In the late 1960s, day-to-day management of the morning and afternoon staffs transferred to executive sports editor Jim Minter, leaving Bisher free to roam and write.

The Atlanta papers merged their newsrooms in 1982, and since then the readers of both have enjoyed Bisher's columns.

Atlanta's papers have been the principal, but not the sole outlet, for Bisher's enormous output. He also has been a columnist for *The Sporting News* and published 1,000-plus stories in magazines including *The Saturday Evening Post, Sport, True,* and others. He moderated the weekly Atlanta television show, "Football Review," from 1950 to 1968.

Bisher is the author of *With a Southern Exposure; Miracle in Atlanta; Strange but True Baseball Stories; Arnold Palmer — The Golden Years; Aaron; The College Game; The Masters; The Furman Bisher Collection* and *Thankful.*

Few U.S. sportswriters have been anthologized as often. His stories and columns have appeared in *Best Sports Stories of the Year, A Treasury of Sports Stories, Sportswriter's Choice* and *The Fireside Book of Football.*

Bisher was president of the Football Writers of America in 1959-60; a charter member of the Atlanta-Fulton County Stadium Authority; first chairman of the Atlanta chapter of the Baseball Writers of America; and president of the National Sportscasters and Sportswriters Hall of Fame, which places your photograph on the wall of the Holiday Inn in Salisbury, N.C., in 1974-76.

Perhaps the most significant juried competitions he has won to date are the AP Sports Editors' Red Smith Award for column writing in 1988 and the Atlanta chapter of the Society of Professional Journalists' Green Eyeshade Award for sports commentary in 1991. He has at least 21 Georgia AP Association sportswriting awards, and others from the Georgia Press Association; the papers have lost count. Bisher also won awards from United Press International while it lived, and the Turf Writing Award of the Florida Thoroughbred Breeders Association in 1972 and 1975.

Bisher was enshrined in the National Sportscasters and Sportswriters Hall of Fame of Salisbury, N.C. in 1989. *Time* magazine in 1961 named him one of the nation's five best columnists. He received the Jake Wade Award of the College Sports Information Directors of America in 1979 for his contributions to college football.

Bisher has given of himself to help the less fortunate in his adopted hometown, serving at various times on the board of directors of the Salvation Army Boys Club; chairman of the Georgia Tuberculosis Association; and chairman of the Georgia Easter Seal Christmas campaign of 1961.

A half-century of careful investments have left him well off, but he wrote this for *Who's Who in America:*

"My good fortune is not to be confused with success, whose definition yet remains vague to me. Success is some mythical goal clamored and struggled for, and whose pursuit is never-ending. One level leads to a requirement to seek another. Success, in my mind, must be related to the status of that person who achieves happiness, and yet may never have been outside his county."

He is married to the former Lynda Landon. Furman has three sons, Roger Bisher, James F. Bisher Jr. and Monte Bisher; two stepdaughters, Patricia McKinney and Samantha McKinney; two step-grandsons, Benjamin Mathis and Adam Mathis; and a grandson, James F. Bisher III.

CELESTINE SIBLEY is in her sixth decade of writing bylined columns and articles for the Atlanta newspapers. At Christmastime 1997, she completes a 56th year as a staff writer, an amazing 52nd as a columnist.

An indefatigable, enduring part of Atlanta's cultural scene, she is responsible for four columns a week. They appear on Monday, Wednesday and Friday on the front of the Living section, and on Sunday in the Dixie Living section.

She was born May 23, 1917 in Holley, Fla., near Pensacola, in the "piney woods" of West Florida, she says, and later moved to Creola, Ala., near Mobile.

Her journalism instinct arose quickly when she served as editor of the school paper at Mobile's Murphy High School. One day the daily *Mobile Press-Register* called looking for students to work on weekends. She nominated herself, and at 15 began her newspaper career. She later attended Spring Hill College in Mobile.

Sibley was a full-time reporter for the *Press-Register* in 1931-36, and for the nearby Pensacola, Fla., *News-Journal* from 1936 to 1941.

She married a *Press-Register* copy editor, James Little. They headed north to land jobs in Atlanta, she as a reporter for *The Constitution*, he with Georgia AP.

In 1945, *The Constitution* asked her to write a personal column. She didn't think much of them, didn't know what she might write about, she told the famed editor, Ralph McGill. In the course of the conversation, she mentioned that her children were having trouble with their tonsils.

"Write about that," McGill said.

She did. Her other subjects for news stories and columns have included 20 years of the Georgia legislature; the movies (she made annual junkets to Hollywood in the early 1950s); important murder trials; and the court proceedings in 1968 to 1971 in Memphis for James Earl Ray, where he pleaded guilty and was convicted of the murder of Dr. Martin Luther King Jr.

Some other staples of her column through the years have been her mother, "Muv" to her readers; Sibley's Sweet Apple cabin north of Atlanta, where she moved in 1963; her getaways to Dog Island, Fla., on the Gulf near Tallahassee; Christmas and preparation for it; gardening; reading; hoboes and eccentrics of the streets of downtown Atlanta; and families.

She once quit for a few days and became a waitress because a stingy comptroller wouldn't reimburse a $25 entry on her expense account. Sibley had a heartbreaking decade in which a son-in-law abducted two of the columnist's grandchildren. (The two who endured that harrowing experience were safely returned to their mother, and today are grown and married.)

Sibley and her office mate and fellow columnist, Harold Martin, were co-stars of the *Constitution* op-ed page for years. The were among the close associates of legendary *Constitution* editor Ralph McGill. He doted on her, once writing, "If there is a queen of our news shop, it is Miss Sibley."

She immortalized the little-known, and was friend to the famous. At an Atlanta Press Club luncheon, Sibley was seated next to "a fat little woman with a crazy hat on." She and author Margaret Mitchell began their friendship.

At Flannery O'Connor's home, Sibley sat on the porch with the eminent author. They watched with amusement as New York publishing representatives arrived and stepped gingerly through the guinea droppings in the yard.

In juried competitions, Sibley has won a 1948 "Pall Mall Big Story" prize for her stories about Floyd Woodward, a man extradited from California to stand trial in Georgia on a murder charge. As a result of Ms. Sibley's articles, Woodward was freed by the Board of Pardons and Paroles. She also received a 1951 Christopher Award, given by the religious organization for her column about her child saying the blessing, which is reprinted here. She has been a winner in Georgia Press Association and Georgia AP contests.

Sibley was honored with the Ralph McGill award of the Atlanta chapter of the Society of Professional Journalists for her contributions to the profession, and received the Townsend Prize for fiction; it is named for a one-time editor of *Atlanta* magazine. Sibley was Atlanta "Woman of the Year" in the Arts in 1956.

Her compassion in the column has benefitted many an organization and family in distress. The Christian Council of Metropolitan Atlanta has been a favorite of hers. She led a fundraising drive for Atlanta Area Services for the Blind, and she has been a member of the Board of Advisors of Grady Hospital and Advisory Board of the Neighborhood Justice Center.

Sibley has had a parallel career as the prolific author of books in the fields of fiction, murder-mystery, and non-fiction. In her successful first book, *The Malignant Heart*, a newsroom employee is killed, stabbed with a copy stake — a plot twist now made unlikely by the advent of computers, which she adjusted to grudgingly but now avidly uses.

The 21 other books in the Sibley library, one of Georgia's largest, are *Peachtree Street USA; Dear Store; Christmas in Georgia; A Place Called Sweet Apple; Especially at Christmas; Mothers Are Always Special; The Sweet Apple*

Gardening Book; Day by Day with Celestine Sibley; Small Blessings; Children, My Children; Young 'Uns and *For All Seasons.*

Also *Jincey; Turned Funny; Tokens of Myself; A Plague of Kinfolks; Dire Happenings at Scratch Ankle; Straight as an Arrow; Ah, Sweet Mystery; The Celestine Sibley Sampler* and *Spider in the Sink.*

Sibley has outlived two husbands, James Little Sr. and Jack Strong. Her children are James Little Jr., Susan Bazemore and Mary Vance. Her grandchildren are Charles "Bird" Fleming, Ted Bazemore, John Bazemore, Susan Bazemore, Sibley Fleming, David Vance, John Steven Vance and Betsy Vance. Her great-grandchildren are Vincent Schaum, Wolfie Schaum and Jack Bazemore.

ACKNOWLEDGMENTS

We gratefully acknowledge the assistance of the following persons in making this project a success:

Sibley Fleming

Ginny Everett and her staff in News Research Services at *The Journal-Constitution*, including Richard Hallman, Cathy High, John Jackson, Kathryn Hulshof, Valerie Lyons, Greg Smith and Dorothy Shea

Atlanta Braves

Atlanta Falcons

National Baseball Hall of Fame and Museum, Cooperstown, New York

Betty Talmadge

John Walter

Deborah Childers

Dave McLean

Lorraine Bennett

Scott Kellogg

Ron Martin

John Walter

Guy Curtright

Amanda Husted